GRANTA BOOKS

WE THE PEOPLE

Timothy Garton Ash is a Fellow of St Antony's College, Oxford, and writes regularly for the *New York Review of Books* and the *Independent*. He is the author of *'Und willst du nicht mein Bruder sein . . .' Die DDR heute* ('And if you won't my brother be . . .' The GDR Today), *The Polish Revolution: Solidarity*, which won the Somerset Maugham Award, and, most recently, *The Uses of Adversity: Essays on the Fate of Central Europe*, which won the European Essay Prize. In 1989 he was also awarded the David Watt Memorial Prize, for his commentaries on international affairs.

ALSO BY TIMOTHY GARTON ASH

The Polish Revolution: Solidarity
The Uses of Adversity

TIMOTHY GARTON ASH

We The People

The Revolution of '89
Witnessed in Warsaw, Budapest, Berlin & Prague

GRANTA BOOKS

CAMBRIDGE
in association with
PENGUIN BOOKS

GRANTA BOOKS
2–3 Hanover Yard, Noel Road, Islington, London N1

Published in association with the Penguin Group
Penguin Books Ltd, 27 Wrights Lane, London W8 5TZ, England
Viking Penguin, a division of Penguin Books USA Inc.
375 Hudson Street, New York, New York 10014, USA
Penguin Books Australia Ltd, Ringwood, Victoria, Australia
Penguin Books Canada Ltd, 2801 John Street, Markham, Ontario, Canada L3R 1B4
Penguin Books (NZ) Ltd, 182–190 Wairau Road, Auckland 10, New Zealand

Penguin Books Ltd, Registered Offices: Harmondsworth, Middlesex, England

First published in Great Britain by Granta Books 1990
3 5 7 9 10 8 6 4

Printed in England by Clays Ltd, St Ives plc
Photoset by Cambridge Photosetting Services

For D., T. & A.

Tvá vláda, lide, se k tobě navrátila!

People, your government has returned to you!

Václav Havel, President of Czechoslovakia, in his 1990 New Year's Address. Havel was adapting words from the seventeenth-century Czech scholar Comenius originally quoted by Tomáš Garrigue Masaryk in his inaugural address as first President of Czechoslovakia, in 1918.

Contents

Witness and History

One day in April 1989 I found myself in the Dimitrov coal-mine at Bytom, in Upper Silesia. The occasion was the first public meeting of Solidarity in this mine since General Jaruzelski declared a 'state of war' in Poland in December 1981, and there was a quiet anger in all the dusty faces. One clean-faced podgy man, wearing a suit, sat incongruously in the first row. He was the Party secretary. After a minute's silence for those—many of them miners—who were killed during the 'state of war', the Solidarity chairman introduced Lech Wałęsa's candidates for election to parliament from the region: a mining engineer, a teacher and the opposition leader and essayist Adam Michnik. The candidates spoke in turn, Michnik observing that this was the first time in their lives that they could vote for an MP of their own choosing. This election, he said, spelled the end of the 'Stalinist-totalitarian system'. The Party secretary clutched his papers with a sweating hand.

Shortly afterwards the Solidarity chairman announced to the assembled miners that there was, in their midst, a visitor from Britain who had written some sort of a book about Solidarity. Then he thrust the microphone into my hand. Taken completely by surprise, I stammered out a speech in which I made, so far as I can recall, three main points. First, I said that I had come there as an independent observer to write about this remarkable election campaign, which had once again drawn the eyes of the world to Poland. Secondly, I said that, as an independent observer, I wanted to tell them that the name of Adam Michnik was well known in the West, and that it had become a synonym for integrity, courage and resistance. Thirdly, I wanted to tell them— as an independent observer—that if they voted for Adam Michnik, and his admirable fellow candidates, then the West would probably give more money to help Poland.

All three statements were strictly true, but I would not deny that, taken together, they might conceivably have been construed as recommending to the audience a certain course of action, or, to put it another way, as 'interference in the internal affairs of the Polish People's Republic'. 'Instant expulsion!' said Bronisław Geremek, the veteran Solidarity adviser, when he heard what had happened. But this time I was not expelled, and by the end of the year there was no longer a Polish *People's* Republic to interfere in. The people had deleted the People.

In any case, thus it was that I came to give the first— and I sincerely hope the last—election speech of my life, in Polish, in a Silesian coal-mine.

A week earlier I had attended, in Budapest, what was described as a 'fête'. An opposition fête. Near the stalls, selling samizdat rather than home-made jam, there was a banner that said simply 'Hyde Park'. In the marquee, a discussion had been organized between the representatives of no less than seven political groups, with the man from the Hungarian Socialist Workers' Party, the ruling communist party, just one among many. There were Free Democrats, Social Democrats, Small-holders, a so-called People's Party, the Hungarian Democratic Forum, and the hosts, the Alliance of Young Democrats. The spokesman for the Free Democrats, a

12

sociologist called Bálint Magyar, said: 'Our programme is to change the system, not to reform it.' The Free Democrats wished to turn the neo-Stalinist dictatorship into a multi-party democracy and to transform the planned economy into a market economy based on private ownership. The loudest applause of the day came when Viktor Orbán, the fiery, black-bearded leader of the Alliance of Young Democrats, declared that Hungary should leave the Warsaw Pact.

Coming out of the marquee I was suddenly sat down behind a rickety table, next to a stall selling samizdat copies of a translation of my recent essays about Central Europe. These I was ordered to sign. Meanwhile the stall-keeper started talking in the sort of jocularly lifted voice that people will use at fêtes when they say 'Roll up for the shove-ha'penny!' or 'Any more for the tombola!'

After many a winter, this was spring. But in April, while a comparison with 1848 had already come to mind, it was the springtime of only two nations, Poland and Hungary. The other four states of what was misleadingly called Eastern Europe were still frozen in various kinds of dictatorship, ranging from Brezhnevite immobility in Czechoslovakia and East Germany to the outright tyranny of Romania's 'socialism in one family'. For me personally, this meant that I was banned from going back to East Germany, and wrote about Czechoslovakia under the pseudonym of Edward Marston, or once, I blush to admit, Mark Brandenburg. (Edward Marston first started writing for the *Spectator* from East Germany in the late 1970s. Now that the files of the State Security Service are reportedly to be made available for scrutiny by scholars, I look forward to studying the one on Marston, E.) An American specialist referred to these

13

unreconstructed states as 'the gang of four'—a description that could well be applied to their leaders, Honecker, Husák, Zhivkov and, last but not least, Ceauşescu.

Even in Poland and Hungary, what was happening could still hardly be described as revolution. It was in fact, a mixture of reform and revolution. At the time, I called it 'refolution'. There was a strong and essential element of change 'from above', led by an enlightened minority in the still ruling communist parties. But there was also a vital element of popular pressure 'from below'. In Hungary, there was rather more of the former, in Poland of the latter, yet in both countries the story was that of an interaction between the two. The interaction was, however, largely mediated by negotiations between ruling and opposition élites.

This story cannot be told in detail here. Yet a few signposts are essential. In both Poland and Hungary, the direct antecedents of the 'refolutions' of 1989 may be traced back to May 1988. Characteristically, in Poland the refolution began with strikes, in Hungary, with a Party conference. That Party conference replaced the ailing János Kádár with Károly Grósz who, being just fifty-seven years old, was naturally hailed in the West as young, pragmatic and dynamic. But what Grósz led over the next year was less a dynamic advance than a confused retreat, in which the Party conceded position after position: by the end of 1988 it was allowing opposition groups to form and to organize demonstrations; in January 1989, legal guarantees of free assembly and association (though not yet for political parties) were passed through parliament; in February, the Party declared its support in principle for the transition to 'a multi-party system', and in April it formally jettisoned the Leninist principle of 'democratic centralism'.

To some extent all this was the result of a deliberate strategy of retreating in order to advance—*reculer pour mieux sauter*. The trouble was, they never got to the *sauter*. Those who did were the various opposition groups and fledgling parties that I saw represented at the fête. Them and the journalists. For this was a movement conducted as much in the media as on the streets. To be sure, there were demonstrations of growing size, notably on the anniversaries of the earlier Hungarian revolutions, 15 March (1848) and 23 October (1956). But even here, the major impact in the country at large came through media reports, and especially through television broadcasts. In sum, there was a curious disproportion between the relatively weak people's 'push' and the Party's 'pull'.

Not so in Poland. Here the story of 1989 can not be understood without reference to the largest and most sustained popular 'push' in the history of communist Eastern Europe, that of Solidarity since 1980. And here the path to the negotiated end of communism began with a further round of strikes, in May 1988, during which the workers chanted, to the dismay of the authorities, to the delight of Solidarity, and somewhat to the surprise of both, *'Nie ma wolności bez Solidarności!'*: There's no liberty without Solidarity.

I spent a day at the birthplace of Solidarity, the Lenin Shipyard in Gdańsk, after being led in by a charming student, over a perimeter wall, under a huge pipe, around the rusting hull of a Soviet ferry, to avoid the riot police who had blockaded the yard. Inside the strike committee headquarters, I found Lech Wałęsa, in striped trousers and leather house slippers, arguing with one of his main advisers, the Catholic editor

Tadeusz Mazowiecki, while half the committee crowded round. Mazowiecki was trying to persuade Wałęsa to throw his authority into the negotiations but Wałęsa was foxily refusing. *'Panie Tadeuszu,'* he said, 'you're the man for negotiations, you're for wisdom!' And Pan Tadeusz cast a wry glance over Wałęsa's shoulder, as if to say 'What can you do with a character like this!'

Later I talked to some of the relatively few workers who had risked occupying the yard. One summed up their grievances in the pithy and far from trivial observation: 'Forty years of socialism and there's still no toilet paper!' When I wished them success, another said, shrugging his shoulders, 'Maybe in thirty years...' That was the feeling, and just thirty hours later the remaining strikers marched out arm-in-arm, Father Henryk Jankowski to Wałęsa's right hand, Mazowiecki to his left, while in front of them someone carried a wooden cross bearing the words 'God, Honour, Country' and underneath '1970, 1980, 1988...'

It looked like a defeat. As late as July 1988, the then government spokesman Jerzy Urban could say that 'the Solidarity movement . . . belongs to the past for good.' But in August there was another wave of strikes, larger than the last, with the strikers still more widely and emphatically demanding the return of Solidarity. On 31 August, the eighth anniversary of the 1980 Gdańsk Agreement that was Solidarity's birth certificate, the interior minister, General Czesław Kiszczak, had a much-publicized and demonstrative meeting with Lech Wałęsa, whom the authorities had so long attempted to ignore as a mere 'private citizen'. Wałęsa then used his personal authority to quell the strikes.

There followed four months of tortuous, often secret negotiation between Solidarity leaders and a group

16

within the Party leadership, while Wałęsa again triumphed in a television debate with the head of the official trade unions, one Alfred Miodowicz. Wałęsa's large group of mainly intellectual advisers also formally constituted itself a 'Citizens' Committee'. Crucially, the party of negotiation won General Jaruzelski's support. Putting all *his* personal authority on the line, he managed to force through the decision to accept the return of Solidarity, at a stormy Central Committee plenum in January 1989. The path was then clear for the unprecedented 'Round Table' talks, which opened on 6 February. The photograph of the huge, bagel-shaped round table, seen from above, with a great bouquet of flowers in the middle, went, as they say, round the world. More to the point, it went round Eastern Europe.

The history of the Round Table, with its sub-tables and sub-sub-tables, its informal summit meetings in the village of Magdalenka near Warsaw, its bizarre conversations between former prisoners and their former gaolers, deserves a separate book. Perhaps the largest historical irony of these talks is that it was the authorities who sought early elections, believing that the shorter the campaign the better their own chance to defeat a wholly unprepared opposition. Solidarity, by contrast, went into the talks determined to get one thing alone: the legal restoration of Solidarity. Beyond that, they would press for fundamental changes in the media, the law, education and local government. Early elections, with agreed restraints, were, they thought, just part of the price they would have to pay. Another part was a strong presidency for General Jaruzelski. In the event, they discovered they could get more than they originally bargained for, and ended up not only with a free contest for thirty-five per cent of the seats in the *sejm,* but also with a free vote for the whole of a new upper house of parliament, the Senate. The first proposal for free elections to the upper chamber actually came from a member of the communist side, during one of those informal summits known colloquially as 'a Magdalenka'.

The Round Table agreement was signed on 5 April. The preamble to this long and complex document declared it to be 'the beginning of the road to parliamentary democracy.' In one of the drafting committees the Party representatives had proposed to introduce a parenthesis after that phrase with words to the effect that 'the government-coalition side regard parliamentary democracy as socialist democracy.' The Solidarity negotiators, after considering their position, said they would agree—so long as a further sentence could be added to the effect that this was also 'the beginning of the building of a sovereign, independent Poland.' The Party negotiatiors then dropped their original suggestion. So much for socialist democracy.

Three weeks later, I found myself rattling up to Gdańsk on the morning express with a buffet-car full of Warsaw's opposition intelligentsia, most of them now officially selected by the Citizens' Committee as candidates for parliament. We were going to the Lenin Shipyard for a meeting of Solidarity's 261 candidates from all over Poland. The meeting was held in the same hall that the inter-factory strike committee had used in August 1980, with the same model ships in glass cases, the same white eagle on the wall, and the same bust of Lenin. As he walked up on to the platform, Lech Wałęsa—the same—gave that Lenin a laughing glance, as if to say, 'So *who whom* to you, old chum.' Later, each candidate had his photograph taken shaking hands with Lech Wałęsa. Two hundred and sixty-one handshakes. The photography was supervised by the film director Andrzej Wajda. My notebook records Bronisław Geremek explaining that these elections were not democratic but 'the key is the hope that in four years there will be free democratic elections.'

Four years! How tame those daring thoughts look now! Yet if nothing more had happened in the last seven months of 1989, what occurred in Hungary and Poland between January and May would have been recorded at year's end as spectacular, unprecedented and historic. In the event, these negotiated breakthroughs, these 'refolutions', became almost forgotten as history started to accelerate at a giddy pace. First, there was Solidarity's own extraordinary triumph in the June elections, which led to the appointment of the first non-communist prime minister in Eastern Europe for forty years. Then there was the reburial in Budapest of the hero of the Hungarian revolution of 1956, Imre Nagy, and the events that led from that to the first formal dissolution of a ruling East European communist party.

Meanwhile, as an unintended, indeed barely considered side-effect of the Hungarian refolution, the 'cutting of the Iron Curtain' between Hungary and Austria allowed a growing number of East Germans to escape across that now 'green' frontier. This was a vital catalyst of the revolution that then erupted to coincide neatly with the fortieth anniversary of the German Democratic Republic. Bulgaria followed with a palace revolution, plus a little help from the streets, but was immediately overtaken by Czechoslovakia. In Prague, late one night and not entirely sober, I told Václav Havel's wife, Olga, that Ceauşescu would be gone before the end of the year. She offered to bet on it—a bottle of

19

champagne. Sober next morning, I thought I had lost a bottle of champagne. But then, just before Christmas . . .

Nobody hesitated to call what happened in Romania a revolution. After all, it really looked like one: angry crowds on the streets, tanks, government buildings in flames, the dictator put up against a wall and shot. It is, however, a serious question whether what happened in Poland, Hungary, Bulgaria or even Czechoslovakia and East Germany, actually qualified for anything but a very loose usage of the term 'revolution'. This doubt was expressed by several intellectuals in the countries concerned. Should popular movements which, however spontaneous, massive and effective, were almost entirely non-violent, really be described by a word so closely associated with violence? Yet the change of government, no, the change of life, in all these other countries was scarcely less profound than in Romania. By a mixture of popular protest and élite negotiation, prisoners became prime ministers and prime ministers became prisoners.

This sudden and sweeping end to an *ancien régime*, and the fact that it occurred in all the countries of Eastern Europe within the space of a few months, may justify the use of the word 'revolution' in my sub-title. My title, the first words of the Constitution of the United States of America, is meant, apart from grabbing the browser's eye, to hint at three notable aspects of these events: the uses but also the ambiguities of the term 'the people' (as, incidentally, with the framing of the US Constitution itself); the fact that, in Hungary, Poland and Czechoslovakia at least, the leaders of the revolutions or refolutions had a startlingly clear idea of the constitutional order they wanted to build, not just of what they wanted to destroy, and this new order bore

not a little resemblance to that established in the
United States (what one might call transatlantic
Europe) two centuries before; and, finally, the sense
that these events, in their rhetoric and street theatre,
somehow themselves belonged to earlier centuries, not
to our common-marketized world.

I cannot emphasize too strongly that this is not a
comprehensive history of the events of 1989 in Eastern
Europe. I do not pretend to offer a full analysis of Soviet
policy, of economic factors, of developments inside the
communist parties and governments, let alone of the
longer-term causes. (Some account of these can be found
in my earlier books, *The Polish Revolution* and *The
Uses of Adversity*, to which this is a sequel.) Even less do
I pretend to make any firm predictions about the future.
To write about 1989 at the beginning of 1990 is perhaps
slightly less foolhardy than to write about 1789 at the
beginning of 1790; but it is foolhardy enough.
 I do not describe events in Bulgaria and Romania,
because I was not there. I was there at important
moments in the other countries, but even here my
account is largely from inside the opposition movements
and from among so-called 'ordinary people' on the
streets—and mainly, as the sub-title indicates, the
streets of the capital cities. The chapter on Prague is
much the longest, because there my vantage-point as a
witness was unique. The disadvantages of the witness as
against the historian are those of partiality in space,
time and judgement. The witness can only be in one
place at one time, and tends to attach an exaggerated
importance to what he personally saw or heard. The
historian can gather all the witnesses's accounts and is
generally unswayed by that first-hand experience.

What happened afterwards changes our view of what went before. The historian usually knows more about what happened afterwards, simply because he writes later. Finally, there is partiality in judgement.

'I am a camera,' said Isherwood. I was not a camera. A camera would not give an election speech in a Silesian coal-mine. Certainly, I have made every effort to get at all the facts, to listen to all sides, to be both fair and critical. But the reader will see that my sympathies are generally with those who made these revolutions rather than with those who attempted to prevent them, with the former prisoners of conscience rather than the former gaolers of conscience.

Few laws are more universal than Acton's 'all power corrupts', and I dare say these countries' new rulers will be corrupted too. To have been persecuted yourself is not necessarily the best protection against the temptation to persecute others. (Many of the communist leaders of Eastern Europe were themselves former political prisoners: Honecker, Husák, Kádár, even Ceauşescu.)

> *I and the public know*
> *What all schoolchildren learn,*
> *Those to whom evil is done*
> *Do evil in return.*

But like most of the inhabitants of East Central Europe I am so conscious of the human price paid under the old evils, and the relief of being rid of them, that my inclination is not immediately to start hunting up new evils.

Such are the grave disadvantages of a witness. But there are also advantages. The witness can, if he is lucky, see things that the historian will not find in any document. Sometimes a glance, a shrug, a chance

remark, will be more revealing than a hundred speeches.
In these events, even more than in most contemporary
history, much of great importance was not written down
at all, either because it occurred in hasty conversations
with no note-takers present, or because the business was
conducted on the telephone, or because the words or
pictures came by television. (The importance of television can hardly be overstated. Future historians of
these events will surely have to spend as much time in
television archives as in libraries.) The witness can see
how things that appear to have been spontaneous were
actually rigged; but also how things that appear to have
been carefully arranged were in fact the hapless product
of sheer confusion. And perhaps the most difficult thing
of all for the historian to recapture is the sense of what,
at a given historical moment, people did *not* know about
the future.

In an attempt to preserve this quality—blissful ignor-
ance, if you will—I have arranged this book in the
following way. The four main chapters contain accounts
of the June elections in Warsaw, the reburial of Imre
Nagy in Budapest, also in June, the opening of the
Berlin Wall, in November, and two weeks of the revolution in Prague, in November and early December.
These are reproduced here substantially as I recorded
them at the time, or very shortly afterwards, in my
notebooks and in articles for the *New York Review of
Books* and the *Spectator*. Each of these chapters ends
with a very brief summary of subsequent developments
to the end of 1989, also drawing, where appropriate, on
first-hand material, but looking back from January
1990. All have the defects, but perhaps also the
qualities, of having been written fresh and fast. The
final chapter is a set of reflections on the revolution,

originally thrown down in note-form for a lecture in December 1989, and substantially rewritten in January 1990.

The book thus has two time-frames: one immediately contemporary, the other looking back from early 1990. The reader will then superimpose his own, third, time-frame, from months or even years later. If things have gone badly in East Central Europe by the time you read this, you will probably find what follows absurdly hopeful and terribly light-hearted. Carefully avoiding all quotations from Wordsworth, I would say only that this, too, belongs to the record. It felt like that at the time.

Warsaw: The First Election

With hindsight it begins to seem obvious that Solidarity should have won a landslide victory on Sunday 4 June, in the first round of the closest thing to a free election that Poland had seen for half a century. They must have known they would win! But they didn't. I sat with an exhausted and depressed Adam Michnik over lunch that Sunday, and he did not know. I drank with a nervously excited Jacek Kuroń late that evening, and he did not know. Nobody knew.

Certainly the campaign had gone well. Despite all the starting handicaps, the lack of organization, money, offices, staff, and, most of all, media, the Solidarity-opposition campaign had become a festival of national improvisation. Despite all the initial advantages, the organization, money, offices, staff and monopoly control of radio and television, the campaign organized by the Polish United Workers' Party and its subordinate coalition partners had been extraordinarily feeble. Solidarity selected just one candidate for each seat it was entitled to contest under the terms of the Round Table agreement. The selection procedure was not democratic, but it was highly effective. The Party-coalition side wasted weeks in quasi-democratic feuding, and ended up with several candidates for most seats, thus ensuring that their vote would be split.

Everywhere walls were covered with the names and faces of the Solidarity candidates. Each was shown in a photograph with Lech Wałęsa, taken at that meeting in the Lenin Shipyard. Underneath was the simple message, in Wałęsa's handwriting, 'We must win.' To find out the names of the Party-coalition candidates, by contrast, often required a lengthy private investigation. Solidarity's posters were red and white, with the unmistakeable jumbly lettering. In several places, the Party had retreated into a faded conservative blue. A typical Party slogan was 'with us it's safer'—a slogan for contraceptives rather than parliamentary candidates, as one Italian observer remarked.

On the day before the vote, I watched Kuroń pacing up and down the stage of the shabby Tęcza Cinema in the working-class borough of Żoliborz, rallying the faithful. First we were shown a long and largely inaudible videotape about the history of the Workers' Defence Committee, KOR, founded in 1976. For much of the audience this was already ancient history. Then Kuroń answered questions. One concerned a central bone of contention in the campaign, control of television. Television, said Kuroń, should be 'public' but not 'governmental'. It should be like the BBC! Then he quoted a revealing remark made by a senior Party official, during the Round Table talks: 'We'll give you the Zomo (riot police) before we give you the TV ' 'And he's quite right,' commented Kuroń, 'I'd much rather have the TV.'

On the overcast Sunday morning I went to the polls in Żoliborz with my indomitable underground publisher, Andrzej Rosner, his wife Ania, and their seven-year-old daughter Zuzia. Ania proudly observed that this was the first time she had gone to vote in her life, since she had boycotted all the ealier, unfree elections. Andrzej confessed that he *had* voted once before—most embarassing—but he had been just eighteen so it hardly counted. A steady stream of people flowed across the barren ground between the half-finished high-rise blocks, dodging huge muddy puddles on their way to vote. Outside the polling station, the only 'information point' was for Solidarity. Inside, it was all official red-and-white: the flag, the posters, even the ballot-boxes.

Andrzej and Ania were handed their complicated ballot papers: separate white ones for each seat in the *sejm*; the 'National List' of thirty-five prominent Party-coalition candidates, who merely had to get more than fifty per cent of the vote to take uncontested seats; and a long pink paper listing all the numerous candidates for the Senate. Ignoring the curtained booths, Andrzej and Ania sat down at a table and began the glorious work of deletion: for, in yet another blunder, the Party-coalition side had insisted that voting should be by crossing out the undesired candidates. Zzzick, zzzick, went the pens, as my friends crossed out name after official name, taking their time about it, savouring the moment. With an access of feminine mercy, Ania left one name out of the thirty-five on the National List—that of a judge who had not, it was suggested, been entirely a swine. Then we walked home, round the giant muddy puddles, past the half-completed blocks, the tenements of communism, in a glow of quiet but profound satisfaction.

It looked much the same all over Warsaw. By mid-morning there were long queues. 'You see, it's after Mass,' was the explanation given me for the length of the queues in almost every case: that and the sheer complexity of the voting procedures. Some voters came directly from their children's First Communion, trailing little girls in long white dresses. The first communion and the first election. And not only for the children. 'Yes, sir,' confided one not-so-young couple, holding hands and simpering, 'it's our first time!' Over the river in Praga, Warsaw's Bronx, schoolchildren watched their classrooms being used as polling stations. The school of democracy. Under their arms, the kids carried rolls of sticky, dirty election posters which they had ripped down from the walls as souvenirs.

In the corridor I was approached by an old man, in some perplexity. 'Excuse me,' he said, 'Byliński—is he ours (*nasz*)?' Yes, I said, he's ours. Zzzick, zzick, went the pen, as he crossed out all the National List, muttering to himself, 'I've had enough of them, all these years . . . ' Then, taking the pink sheet, 'And Findeisen, is he ours?' Yes, he's ours. 'And Trzeciakowski, where is he?' We scanned the closely printed sheet together. At which point a clucking Electoral Commission secretary came up to me and asked, with nervous aggression, 'What role are you playing here?'—as if I might reply, 'An agent of imperialism.'

In the evening I visited the aged printshop of the Party daily, *Trybuna Ludu*, which now also handled the Solidarity-opposition's hastily improvised daily, *Gazeta Wyborcza*, that is 'The Election Paper'. The hot-metal technology was almost Dickensian, but the most interesting part was the on-site censor. Greatly to my delight, the editors of *Gazeta* allowed me to take a cartoon in for approval. Knocking on the door of the censor's office, I stepped in and, as instructed, said in a bored, offhand sort of tone, 'Evenin', *Gazeta Wyborcza*, page five'. Instead of some sinister character in dark glasses I found myself confronted by a woman dressed like a cleaning lady, in a cheap floral dress, with a glass of tea and a fag hanging from her lower lip. This was the censor. She took the proof copy of the cartoon, carefully scanned the article to which it related, presumably for subversive content—though also, I felt, to demonstrate

28

that she could read—and then, marking the back of the cartoon, handed it back to me dismissively, and returned to her glass of tea. Bowing, I gratefully took my leave. Even then—not knowing what the next months would bring—I felt that I had been privileged to witness a minor rite of some endangered tribe, like the yopposnorting of the Yanomami.

Later, I had a drink with Jacek Kuroń, who passed the time before his results came in by giving a hilarious account of his first trip to the United States, and his meeting with President Bush. What did Bush tell him? 'He said he was for democracy. I said, "Me too."'

Next morning I was woken shortly before eight by a telephone call from Janusz Onyszkiewicz, Solidarity's national spokesman through all the long dark years since 1981. He had been elected to parliament, and it looked as if across the country they had won a famous victory. Throughout the day, the news got better and better. The Warsaw Citizens' Committee had its headquarters in a café called, suitably enough, Café Surprise. The first floor contained a whole bank of computer screens, tabulating the latest results.

By the afternoon, Solidarity leaders knew that they had swept the board: winning outright, on the first round, all but a handful of the seats for which they were competing. Three things happened at once: the communists lost an election; Solidarity won; the communists acknowledged that Solidarity won. That might sound like a syllogism. Yet until almost the day before, anyone who had predicted these events would have been universally considered not a logician but a lunatic. Moreover, the three things, while logically related, were also separate and distinct.

First, and above all, the communists lost. They did

not lose power. They still had the army, the police, the Party apparatus and the *nomenklatura*. But they lost the vote. While virtually all the Solidarity candidates got through on the first round, most of the Party-coalition candidates had to go through to a run-off in the second round on 18 June. Most humiliating of all, only two of the thirty-five candidates on the National List got the requisite fifty per cent of valid votes on an uncontested ballot. In other words, more than half of those who turned out to vote took the trouble to cross out, name by name or with one big cross, the prime minister, the interior minister, and the defence minister, as well as other less prominent establishment figures.

Secondly, Solidarity won. Solidarity won not only against the Party, but also against many quite well-known, even distinguished counter-candidates: successful managers, television personalities, representatives of more radical opposition groups, and, most formidably, Christian Democrats enjoying the explicit support of senior churchmen—indeed, of the most senior. For on the very eve of the election the Primate, Cardinal Józef Glemp, made a show of receiving the Christian Democrats standing against Adam Michnik and Jacek Kuroń —both official Solidarity-opposition candidates, but both very much from what Michnik once called the 'lay left'. Yet despite that extraordinary intervention, the Solidarity men still won hands down. 'The Primate should submit his resignation,' murmured the wits.

You might think that Solidarity need not have worried about its popularity. But worry it did. Most opinion polls suggested a fragmentation of the non-communist vote. And whatever the historical legitimacy from 1980–81; whatever the spiritual legitimacy that came from the blessing of the Pope (one up on the Primate); whatever the cultural legitimacy that came from the film stars and winners of the Nobel Prize; whatever the trade-union legitimacy that came from last year's strikes; there is nothing, but nothing, to match the legitimacy that comes from the barrel of the ballot-box.

There was only one opponent that Solidarity did not defeat. He might be called, by analogy with General Winter, General Abstention. All sides in the campaign had agreed on one thing: that everyone should turn out to vote. Yet the final turn-out was very modest: just over sixty-two per cent, which according to the (unreliable) official figures was actually less than the turn-out for a referendum on economic reform in 1987. Perhaps a few people followed radical opposition appeals to boycott even these elections, because they were not wholly free. Perhaps some tepid Party faithful felt so disgusted that they stayed at home. But my own straw polls suggested that the main reason was a deep tiredness and disbelief in the capacity of any political force—red, white or blue—to reverse the country's desperate material decline.

The third thing that happened was, in its way, almost as remarkable. The Party told the truth. On the Monday evening, when the first results were known, the spokesman for the Central Committee, Jan Bisztyga, appeared on the television evening news, sitting side by side with Solidarity's Janusz Onyzszkiewicz, and Mr Bisztyga said: 'The elections had a plebiscitary character and Solidarity won a clear majority.' He said other things too. For example: 'If triumphalism and adventurism anarchize the situation in Poland, democracy and social peace will be seriously threatened.' (Why, one might almost have mistaken that for a threat.) But as the first

31

reaction of a party which had monopolized power for more than forty years, and fought Solidarity tooth and nail for more than seven, this was big. Two days later General Jaruzelski said simply: 'It was the first time that voters could choose freely. That freedom was used for the crossing-off of those who were in power till now.'

Sunday, 4 June 1989 was a landmark not only in the post-war history of Poland, not merely in the history of Eastern Europe, but in the history of the communist world. Yet as they plunged into fevered discussions, negotiations and late-night cabals, the reaction of Solidarity leaders was a curious mixture of exaltation, incredulity and alarm. Alarm at the new responsibilities that now faced them—the problems of success—but also a sneaking fear that things could not continue to go so well. That fear was heightened by the news from China, for the massacre of students demonstrating for democracy on Tiananmen Square occurred on the same day. It was an uncanny experience to watch, with a group of Polish opposition journalists, on the very afternoon of the election, the television pictures from Peking. Martial law. The tanks. The tear-gas. Corpses carried shoulder-high. We had been here before: in Gdańsk, in Warsaw.

As Solidarity leaders began to engage in real politics, with all its evasions, compromises and half-truths, many had mixed feelings. There was more than a touch of nostalgia for the simple truths and moral clarities of the martial law period. One might passionately wish Poland to have 'normal' politics. But it was quite another thing to watch your own friends starting to behave like normal politicians. Yet what is the alternative? Came the answer: 'Tiananmen Square.'

Following its election triumph, Solidarity faced several major questions: the internal structure of the opposition movement, the nature, timing and terms of its participation in government, and its response to the deepening economic crisis. What was Solidarity in the summer of 1989? It was at least four things. First, it was Lech Wałęsa, whose personal popularity and authority had reached extraordinary heights, reinforced, of course, by every meeting with a President Mitterand or Bush. Second, it was the parliamentary group—161 out of 460 members of the *sejm*, ninety-nine out of 100 members of the Senate. These new parliamentarians personally represented very different tendencies and traditions, but on 4 June they were all—social democrat or conservative, Christian or Jew, bright or dull— elected because they were the candidates of Lech Wałęsa and Solidarity. Defeated communist candidates re- marked bitterly that if a monkey had stood as an official Solidarity-opposition candidate he would have been elected; and there is probably some truth in that. One might add that if Saint Paul had stood as a candidate for the Polish United Workers' Party, he would probably have been defeated.

Third, Solidarity was the loose structure of national, regional and local Citizens' Committees which actually organized the election campaign. Beside veteran Soli- darity activists these Citizens' Committees were joined by many people—doctors, engineers, teachers, journal- ists—who had not been so active before. They were the essential constituency organizations for the new mem- bers of parliament, and, as it were, the local nurseries of Poland's seedling democracy. Finally, there was Solidarity as what it had been first: a trade union. But Solidarity-as-trade union had grown only sluggishly since its (re-)registration in April. There was none of the exuberant dynamism of autumn 1980, when an estimated three million people joined the newborn union within a fortnight. In mid-June, after two months, its membership was estimated at between one and a half and two million, and no one imagined it would reach the ten million of 1981. To put it another way, only about one in seven of those who voted for Solidarity-opposition candidates on 4 June had chosen to join the trade union Solidarity. In the best case, the relationship between these four faces of Solidarity would take some time to work out.

One source of repeated controversy was Lech Wałęsa's own high-handed, indeed some said 'dictatorial' style of leadership, both within the trade union and in the wider political arena. Even in Solidarity's first period of legal existence, in 1980 and 1981, Wałęsa had a somewhat ambivalent attitude to democracy inside the movement, and this tendency was not weakened by his singular elevation to the status of a Nobel Prize winner and international statesman. But now as then he countered with a strong practical argument. In an interview for the first issue of the revived *Solidarity Weekly* he asked, rhetorically, 'Can you steer a ship through a stormy sea in a wholly democratic way?'

Increasingly his personal role-model seemed to be Marshal Józef Piłsudski, who first fought for Poland's independence and then, for a decade after his coup of 1926, presided over the independent Polish Republic in distinctly authoritarian fashion. 'Really we should start by singing "We, the First Brigade",' I heard Wałęsa tell the first meeting of the newly elected Solidarity-opposition parliamentarians, referring to the stirring marching song of Piłsudski's Legions in the First World

War. But when he went on to lay down, *de haut en bas*, what should be the form and leadership of a parliamentary group of which he was not even a member, there was instant revolt. This is 'a sort of coup d'état', they said, we really cannot start building democracy with these 'Bolshevik methods'. Wałęsa instantly retreated: 'I like democracy, I love democracy,' he protested. And as it was in that meeting, so it would be in the succeeding years and larger struggles. Wałęsa would like to be a strong leader. There was an objective need for strong leadership. There might also, one might speculate, be some subjective desire for a strong leader. The authoritarian style which went down so badly with democratic activists might actually commend him to a wider public.

Yet where Piłsudski was surrounded by colonels, Wałęsa was surrounded by professors. Where pre-war Poland operated in a Europe of dictatorships, Poland now looked towards a Western Europe of liberal democracies. At his right hand Wałęsa had the sage Professor Bronisław Geremek, a delightful mixture of Macaulay and Machiavelli, and a man who knew exactly what was needed for a modern, Western, European Poland.

At this first meeting of the 'first brigade', conducted behind closed doors in the main auditorium of Warsaw University, Geremek was elected chairman of the joint group of Solidarity-sponsored members of both houses of parliament. When he took the chair, the meeting suddenly acquired both pace and order. Almost the first issue up for discussion was the name the group should give itself. Wałęsa himself insisted—against the pleading of some present—that the title should not include the word 'Solidarity'. He argued that it must be open to all independent, democratic tendencies in Poland.

There were now different tendencies, he said, and in future the differences would widen, as indeed they must, if Poland were to become a real democracy. Various alternative names were proposed, and the resulting acronyms were tried out on the university blackboard. My notes say: 'OKP, OKOP, DKO, KO, OK, OKO.' Eventually they settled on OKP, that is, the Citizens' Parliamentary Club.

At this moment, in mid-June, Solidarity leaders described their ideal timetable—what Polish planners call a 'harmonogram'—for the transition to democracy roughly as follows. For the next year or two they would work as a both a parliamentary and an extra-parliamentary opposition: controlling the conduct of a more competent but still Party-led government, introducing new legislation in many fields, opening up the mass media, reforming the legal system, and building up their grass-roots constituency organization as well as the trade-union Solidarity. After a year or two, they would have free local government elections. These would bring an end to the inefficient, bureaucratic and corrupt *nomenklatura* domination of those vital lower rungs of Polish public life. Meanwhile, a sort of permanent, informal Magdalenka between top Party and Solidarity leaders would resolve the most contentious issues.

Within four years—as agreed at the Round Table— there would then be fully free elections to the national parliament. At this point it would be reasonable to expect the formation of a non-party government. Continuity and Soviet acceptance would be guaranteed by President Jaruzelski, elected for six years. However, with a good dose of optimism and fantasy, it was possible to imagine Wałęsa being elected president in 1995, and then presiding over a regime which, while centralized and even authoritarian at the top, none the less allowed both multi-party democracy and a mixed ownership, free-market economy to grow underneath. In short, Wałęsa would be to Poland what De Gaulle was to France. Thus the dream harmonogram, all other things being equal.

But all other things were not equal, neither externally nor internally. The internal problem was that Solidarity was being sucked into power faster than it wanted to go. It faced choices that it never expected to face. Solidarity leaders insisted that when the terms of the new presidency were being negotiated at the Round Table, the name of General Jaruzelski was never explicitly mentioned in connection with that post. But if it was not explicitly mentioned this was because any schoolboy could see that the post had been designed for him. That was the deal. And the agreed distribution of seats in parliament seemed to guarantee his election.

Yet no one, neither Solidarity nor the Party, reckoned with the sheer scale of Solidarity's victory and the Party-coalition's defeat. When some members of the previously compliant coalition parties, the Democratic Party and the United Peasants Party, let it be known that they did not want to vote for Jaruzelski, Solidarity found itself in the horrifying position of apparently being able to prevent Jaruzelski being elected president. Their own supporters would never forgive them if they voted for Jaruzelski. The army, police, Party apparatus and probably Moscow would not settle for a non-Party candidate. What on earth were they to do? And so we had the surreal spectacle of people who had been interned and imprisoned by General Jaruzelski during martial law now racking their brains to think how they could secure his election as president.

At the same time, the visible economy took a further turn for the worse. A series of price rises which had been delayed until after the election was introduced: sugar, alcohol, petrol, in quick succession. Seeing further price rises ahead, people indulged in panic buying. Shop shelves were cleared. The free-market exchange rate for the dollar soared to the unprecedented level of more than 6,000 Złotys—thus making the average wage, at the free-market exchange rate, just five pounds a month. A projected wage and price freeze was shattered almost before it had been announced. Inflation was soaring into treble figures. It could not go on like this.

After the election, only a government with Solidarity's clear endorsement would have the credibility to push through the painful measures of austerity and restructuring which necessarily would accompany any serious programme of economic reform. As Presidents Mitterand and Bush and Mrs Thatcher all made clear, the West, to which all sides now looked as a *deus ex machina*, would offer substantial debt relief and modest direct help for the private sector even in these chaotic circumstances, but it would—indeed could—only offer large-scale IMF and World Bank programmes to a properly constituted government with a credible economic policy.

Solidarity leaders said they were unprepared for such a role, practically as well as psychologically. Their economists had outline programmes—worse, they had several competing programmes, ranging from the radical liberal to the 'socialist market'—but they had not, could not have, the practical detail which could only be obtained by sitting inside the ministries. But those ministries, and the whole pyramid of bureaucracy beneath them, were still wholly occupied by the Party placemen—the *nomenklatura*. To enter government while those basic structures remained unchanged would be, they said, to condemn yourself to failure. To change those structures required time. But time is what they did not have. They had won the election. The country needed them—now.

And the country got them, but not immediately. First, the combined houses of parliament had to elect a president. Would Jaruzelski scrape home? The suspense lasted a whole month after the second round of the election. Finally, on 19 July, the general was elected by a margin of just one vote. The only reason that he won was that seven Solidarity-opposition members of parliament deliberately cast invalid votes, so as to ensure his victory, while several more abstained. Many Solidarity supporters were furious. But the political brains of the movement argued that this was the best possible result. Jaruzelski had to be elected. That was the deal, and the organs he led, Party, army and police, still held the real power in the land. On the other hand, his election by the smallest possible margin—and visibly by grace of Solidarity—showed unmistakeably who had the real legitimacy in the land. (In fact, in a conversation on the day after the 4 June election, one of the best of those political brains, who in the circumstances had best remain nameless, anticipated precisely this result. If it looks as if the president will not get the necessary majority, he said, 'some of us will just have to get 'flu.')

While a plenum of the chronically disunited Polish United Workers' Party settled on the *soi-disant* 'liberal' Mieczysław F. Rakowski—another of the West's faded darlings—to succeed him as Party leader, Jaruzelski invited another communist general, Czesław Kiszczak, to form a 'grand coalition' government including Solidarity. Kiszczak had been a key figure in the negotiated breakthrough symbolized by the Round Table. But he had also been interior minister thoughout the martial law period. Were Solidarity's leaders now to serve under their former gaoler? Who won the election anyway? Kiszczak himself had been on the National List, and had failed to be elected. 'I welcome you to the *sejm*,' he said to Adam Michnik at a meeting shortly after the election. 'No, General,' said Michnik, 'in the *sejm* I do the greeting!' None the less, several of Solidarity's key strategists, and notably Michnik himself, were at this point thinking in terms of a strategic alliance with communist reformers. Lech Wałęsa came up with an alternative proposal: a 'small coalition', not with the communists, but with the formerly puppet Democratic and United Peasants' parties, most of whose deputies were all too ready to abandon their puppetmasters and establish some credibility before really free elections. Between them they would have a majority in parliament, for under the terms of the Round Table agreement, the communists only had thirty-eight per cent of seats in the *sejm*.

After another fortnight of frantic negotiation, General Kiszczak graciously admitted that he could not form a government, and President Jaruzelski graciously invited Tadeusz Mazowiecki to try to do so. The chalice thus passed from the gentleman-gaoler to the gentleman-prisoner, for Mazowiecki, like most of the top Solidarity leadership, had been interned for a year under martial law. Wałęsa had let it be known that he was considering three candidates for the job,

Mazowiecki, Kuroń and Geremek (while, according to some insiders, privately rather wanting the job himself). Mazowiecki was less of an obvious political rival to Wałęsa than Geremek, and as a devout though liberal Catholic he was also more acceptable to the Church. He would try to build not a small but a large coalition, including communist members in key posts.

At the time no one knew whether Moscow would accept this arrangement. Despite the fine general statements contained, most recently, in Gorbachev's speech to the Council of Europe at Strasbourg in July, there was some ominous huffing and puffing from *Pravda* and *Izvestia*. Reportedly crucial in determining both the Party's and Moscow's attitude was a telephone conversation between Gorbachev and the new Polish Party leader, Rakowski, on 22 August. (Once again, I wonder if future historians will find any written record of this important moment.) By the time Mazowiecki was confirmed by the *sejm* on 24 August, with the votes of most of the communist deputies, it was clear that the Party was ready in principle to serve under him.

After a further three weeks of still more fraught, tortuous and exhausting negotiations, Mazowiecki was able to present his new government to parliament on 12 September. At one point he had to take a break and a walk in the Łazienki gardens, so exhausted was he by the previous month's exertions. 'I come,' he said, 'as a member of Solidarity, faithful to the heritage of August,' and he ended his speech with the words: 'I believe that God will help us to take a great step along the road that now opens before us.' These words were faithfully reprinted in the Party daily, *Trybuna Ludu*, giving God his due initial capital. That paper also gave the traditional potted biographies of the cabinet. Here

Jacek Kuroń, as Minister for Labour and Social Policy, would sit beside Czesław Kiszczak, who remained Minister of the Interior. The Party had retained the all-important interior and defence ministries, but it had surrendered the foreign ministry to a non-party independent, Professor Krzysztof Skubiszewski, a respected international lawyer.

Yet the most important posts of all were the economic ones. For throughout this desperately slow, painful process of negotiated political transition—of refolution —the economic situation had been getting worse, and worse, and worse. The roots of Poland's economic woes could be traced back much further: nearly twenty years, for example, to the beginnings of the ill-fated Gierek experiment, or forty years, to the imposition of full Stalinism, or fifty years, to the German invasion of September 1939. But there is no doubt that Poland paid an additional economic price for being the ice-breaker of political transition. This was true, in a larger sense, throughout the 1980s, and, in a narrower sense, from the spring of 1988. For it was in this period, as all political controls weakened (including those on wage demands), and as Poland's last communist government made increasingly irresponsible moves (notably the decision to free agricultural prices without first creating the free market to regulate them), that inflation soared to appalling heights, from some sixty-four per cent in 1988 to some 640 per cent in 1989.

Among Solidarity's economic spokesmen during the Round Table and the election campaign, the cautious, gradualist 'market socialist' approach had been predominant. The new prime minister was himself deeply influenced by the social teaching of the Pope, and had inclined, in his early days, to believe in the possibility of

Christian socialism. Yet almost the first remark he made as prime minister was: 'I am looking for my Ludwig Erhard!' He found him in a radical liberal economist called Leszek Balcerowicz—an Erhard without the cigar—and the team they assembled included two of the most outspoken advocates of free-market economics and privatization in Poland, the new industry minister, Tadeusz Syryjczyk, and the new housing minister, Aleksander Paszyński.

The Balcerowicz team got to work with exemplary speed, setting out to make up, not just for fifty lost days but for fifty lost years. Within a fortnight, Balżerowicz presented to the finance ministers of the Western world, at an IMF meeting in Washington the outline of their plan 'to transform the Polish economy into a market economy'. Within just three months, on 17 December, he presented to the Polish parliament a balanced budget and a package of eleven laws designed to lay the foundations of the Polish economy for the next half-century. Although it was Christmas-time and MPs grumbled, they got the package through all the readings in just twelve days, so that Poland's 'big bang' could start on the first day of the new decade. In the intervals, they queued up to break the traditional Christmas wafer with the Primate, singing carols as they waited. The Solidarity daily, *Gazeta Wyborcza*, recorded that the Party MPs sang loudest of all. Oh yes, and while they were about it, they dropped the People from the name of the state—changing it back to the time-honoured Polish Republic—and put the crown back on the Polish eagle.

The crucial test of the economic transition was yet to come. But this first phase of *political* transition was quite remarkably peaceful, pragmatic and harmonious.

43

Having fought each other for nearly a decade, Solidarity and Party leaders now worked side-by-side with little more rancour than you would find between the players of two rival football teams. Most of the central bureaucracy stayed in place, and worked loyally, even eagerly for its new masters.

As I discovered when I visited my friend Henryk Woźniakowski, a Catholic intellectual now catapulted into the office of Deputy Government Spokesman— three telephones on the desk, the secretary saying '*Panie Dyrektorze*'!—the only major innovation they made in the Council of Ministers' building was a table-tennis room. As Wałęsa had said: 'It may not be better, but at least it will be more fun . . . ' Sitting in the canteen one could hardly tell *nomenklatura* and Solidarity officials apart, except, perhaps, that the latter looked more uncomfortable in their suits and ties. ('It robs me of half my intellectual capacity,' said Jacek Kuroń, and reverted to his open shirts and jeans.)

In just three months, Polish politics suddenly became normal instead of 'normalized'. In place of the familiar political scene of the 1980s with its three great actors, Authorities, Solidarity, Church, there was a new scene in which the main actors were Government, Parliament, the Presidency, and, as wild card and President-in-waiting, Lech Wałęsa. And the government had started to govern. This may sound usual, but it had not happened in Poland for at least fifty years.

Many observers had suggested that the trade-union or workers' movement character of the Polish opposition —of Solidarity—would be a major disadvantage when it came to making the transition to a market economy. For the people who would suffer most from this transition would be, precisely, the workers, and especially

44

unskilled workers in the huge loss-making Stalinist combines which had been Solidarity's strongholds. In the second half of 1989, however, the oppposite seemed to be the case. As a trade union, Solidarity was now weak: having barely two million members at the end of the year. But the heritage of Solidarity was a priceless advantage.

The prime minister, the labour minister, the head of the Citizens' Parliamentary Club, the chief editor of *Gazeta Wyborcza*, not to mention Lech Wałęsa, were quite unquestionably men of Solidarity. If they now appealed to the workers—'Don't strike! Accept factory closures! Take a real cut in wages!'—they had a better chance of being listened to than anyone else, just because the workers knew that these men, above all others, had fought for their rights over the last ten years. Jacek Kuroń, in particular, made marvellously direct and heart-warming appeals to the public in a regular weekly television chat. (As he had said in his pre-election meeting: rather the TV than the Zomo.) During the first months of its existence, the Mazowiecki government was in the unique position of finding its popularity increasing as prices increased. In a poll conducted on 4 January 1990, fifty-seven per cent of those asked found the government's record 'good or very good' while no less than fifty per cent declared themselves now in favour of the proposed 'shock cure' for the economy. Whether that popularity would survive the shock was, of course, another question.

One day in October a very pretty actress called Joanna Szczepkowska was invited to appear on Polish Television News. She had an announcement to make. 'Ladies and Gentlemen,' she said, 'on 4 June 1989, communism in Poland ended.' It was nice to have a pretty girl saying such things, especially on Polish Television News. But was it true? 'I don't know if I would have delivered such a communiqué myself,' said the sage Professor Bronisław Geremek, 'but it's the plain truth, and I entirely agree with her.' At the time we did not know it, although perhaps we smelled it. But looking back from January 1990, we can see that this was the turning-point. To say that communism in Poland ended on that day was a poetic exaggeration. But the end of communism in Poland followed directly from the free vote of the Polish people on that glorious fourth of June. And perhaps not just in Poland . . .

Budapest: The Last Funeral

In Poland it was an election. In Hungary it was a funeral: the funeral of Imre Nagy, just thirty-one years after his death. Exactly a year earlier, when opposition activists held a demonstration to mark the anniversary of Nagy's execution on 16 June, they had been violently dispersed by the police. Now those same police assisted opposition activists in preparing an extraordinary, ceremonial reburial of the hero of 1956.

Everyone knows that Russian tanks crushed that revolution, setting the pattern of Soviet responses (and Western non-responses) to East European revolutions for the next thirty years. But Hungarians recalled the special perfidy of Nagy's execution: how he and his closest associates were lured out of their refuge in the Yugoslav embassy by a solemn, written undertaking from János Kádár, only to be carried off by Soviet security forces, deported to Romania, returned to Hungary, kept in solitary confinement, subjected to a gross parody of a trial, and then hanged. They also remembered how, for thirty years, the man directly responsible for Nagy's execution, János Kádár, the state and party he led, the newspapers and the school-books, just lied, lied, lied about it all. It was a popular memory all the more potent for being so long repressed.

One of the few defendants who survived the Nagy trial and lived on in Budapest to see this day was Miklós Vásárhelyi. A quiet-spoken, smiling, slightly crumpled figure, Vásárhelyi had been Nagy's adviser and press spokesman during the revolution. In the 1980s he

47

became a sort of elder statesman to the fledgling democratic opposition, well-known to Western visitors but also keeping in touch with senior Party members. Together with the relatives of the executed men, and other insurgents and activists who had survived their time in prison, he watched and waited. By befriending a prison guard he eventually found out that the mortal remains of Nagy and his comrades had been buried in an unmarked grave on Plot 301, the remotest corner of an outlying cemetery. So long as János Kádár was in full control, there was no chance of justice, even retrospectively: to clear Nagy would be to indict Kádár. Indeed, according to an account by one usually reliable source, when two of Kádár's protégés had tried to persuade him to resign, he shouted at them: 'You know what would happen! Within months they would rehabilitate László Rajk, and within a year, Imre Nagy!' Although the West sung his praises, and the world had long forgotten that ancient history, Kádár remembered. He was Macbeth, and Nagy was Banquo.

In the spring of 1988, with Kádár very clearly on the way out, the relatives and survivors established a Committee for Historical Justice. On the thirtieth anniversary of the murder, they held a small, dignified ceremony at Plot 301, but the subsequent demonstration in the centre of town was broken up by the police. Yet the new Party leaders saw the imperative of rehabilitating Nagy if they were ever to gain lasting credibility. If they did not, the shadow of '56 would always be upon them. So in January the government announced that it had decided to allow the exhumation, identification and decent reburial of the remains. Two days later, Imre Pozsgay again forced the pace of political change by trailing the results of a Central Committee subcommittee established to re-evaluate the last forty years (!), and pronouncing 1956 to have been not, as previously maintained, a 'counter-revolution', but rather a 'popular uprising against an oligarchic rule that had debased the nation.'

It was, however, not the Party or government leadership who organized the reburial. It was the Committee for Historical Justice, in association with the main opposition groups (but also in private consultation with Pozsgay and other leading reformist politicians). The Committee declared this to be the day of Imre Nagy's 'ceremonial burial and political resurrection'. It appealed emphatically for calm and dignity. No political banners should be carried, only flags in the national colours or in black. The occasion should not be exploited for disturbances of any kind.

In the days before there was none the less great nervousness among officials of the Hungarian People's Republic. They were afraid of the people.

Heroes' Square, 16 June 1989. The great neo-classical columns are wrapped in black cloth. From the colonnades hang huge red, green and white national flags, but each with a hole in the middle, a reminder of how the insurgents of 1956 cut out the hammer and sickle from their flags. Ceremonial flames burn beside the six coffins ranged on the steps of the temple-like Gallery of Art: five named coffins for Imre Nagy and his closest associates, the sixth, a symbolic coffin of the Unknown Insurgent. A varnished wooden structure shaped like the prow of a schooner juts out from one side. The whole setting has been designed by the opposition activist and architect László Rajk, son of the victim of one of the most notorious Stalinist show trials—another piece of

49

hidden symbolism. Just off one corner of the square is the Yugoslav embassy where Nagy vainly took refuge.

Funeral music sounds from the loudspeakers as people queue under the burning sun to lay flowers in tribute to their martyrs. First come ordinary citizens, quietly placing one or two carnations. They are followed by the official delegations with large, formal wreaths: local councils, churchmen, diplomats, a delegation from Warsaw for Polish-Hungarian Solidarity and senior reformist Hungarian Party politicians, formally representing the government and the parliament, but not— emphatically not—the Party as such.

Then the speeches, including an ancient recording of one of Nagy's wireless appeals from 1956. 'You have just heard the words of Imre Nagy,' says Miklós Vásárhelyi, a remote figure on the pulpit shaped like a schooner's prow, and then he recalls the magic moment before the second and final Soviet intervention (on 4 November), when 'the weapons became silent, no more brotherly blood was shed, and the process of reconciliation and democratic transformation began.' He pleads for 'mutual tolerance and indulgence towards those who are thinking and acting in different ways, for only thus can we ... secure the peaceful transition to a European, modern, free and democratic society.'

'Will freedom for Hungary grow from the blood of these heroes?' asks Sándor Rácz, head of the Budapest Workers' Councils in 1956. There are, he says, three obstacles. The first obstacle is the presence of Soviet troops on Hungarian soil. Then there is the communist party, clinging to power. The third obstacle is the fragmentation of society. Another survivor invites everyone to join hands and declaim the words of Sándor

Petőfi, the poet of 1848: 'No more shall we be slaves!' 'No more shall we be slaves!' they intone.

Yet the crowd, perhaps some 200,000 strong, is still quiet, subdued, when the last speaker takes the stand. 'Citizens!' cries the raven-haired Viktor Orbán of the Young Democrats, 'Forty years ago, although starting from Russian occupation and communist dictatorship, the Hungarian nation just once had a chance, and the strength and courage to try to realize the aims of 1848 . . . ' 'We young people,' he went on, 'fail to understand a lot of things about the older generation . . . We do not understand that the very same party and government leaders who told us to learn from books falsifying the history of the revolution now vie with each other to touch these coffins as if they were lucky charms. We do not think there is any reason for us to be grateful for being allowed to bury our martyred dead. We do not owe thanks to anyone for the fact that our political organizations can work today.' People applaud, as if this is what they have been waiting for. 'If we can trust our souls and strength, we can put an end to the communist dictatorship; if we are determined enough we can force the Party to submit itself to free elections; and if we do not lose sight of the ideals of 1956, then we will be able to elect a government that will start immediate negotiations for the swift withdrawal of Russian troops.' The crowd is finally roused to fierce and prolonged applause. Everything is shown live on national television.

Later, a smaller group travels by bus to the outlying cemetery, where, at the wish of the relatives, the martyrs are to be reburied in the same place where they had lain unidentified for nearly thirty years. I go in company with some Young Democrats, and Adam Michnik, who is here to represent Polish-Hungarian

51

Solidarity. The incorrigible Michnik cheerfully makes the V-for-Victory sign out of the bus window, and a couple of Young Democrats rather self-consciously follow his example. Most of the passers-by look bewildered, but a few do wave back, grinning furtively.

I visited the now legendary Plot 301 just after last year's ceremony. I still have my amateur photographs of the large rubbish dump which then occupied the ground that is now at last prepared for decent burial. They have laid a new road to Plot 301, and lined it with a guard of honour. Along the dusty bulldozed verges, the men in their brown and red uniforms stand incongruously on concrete blocks, like tin soldiers complete with their bases. Around the plot, in the places where a corpse could be identified, they have erected rough-hewn wooden grave-posts, with the tops carved not into crosses but into traditional Hungarian forms. There is a curious atmosphere here, partly because people stand around having more or less ordinary, political conversations while the speakers go on and on, but also due to the almost complete lack of Christian symbolism, ritual or language.

Nagy is often quoted as having declared at his trial: 'I wonder if the people who now sentence me to death won't be the ones who will rehabilitate me later.' Miklós Vásárhelyi testifies that this is a myth. What Nagy did say was that the final words in the case would be spoken by the Hungarian people, history and the international workers' movement. Well, the international workers' movement no longer exists, but the Hungarian people and history have spoken. According to the account Vásárhelyi subsequently pieced together from fellow prisoners and former gaolers, Imre Nagy spent most of his last night writing. 'His letter or notes were never

forwarded to his wife. All she got back from the prison
was a wedding-ring, which turned out to be a fake.'

One name is not mentioned in any of the speeches,
although it is in everyone's mind. It is that of János
Kádár, and Kádár remembered not as the leader of the
West's favourite 'liberal' communist country in the
1970s, but as the traitor who took over from Nagy on
the back of Soviet tanks, the man who was directly
responsible for the murder of Imre Nagy. Where is he
today, that sick old king? Is he watching on television?
Does he see Banquo's ghost lying in state on Heroes'
Square? This is not the funeral of Imre Nagy. It is his
resurrection, and the funeral of János Kádár.

That is what I thought at the time. Next day, there
were rumours that Kádár and his wife had committed
suicide as Imre Nagy was finally laid to rest. In fact
Kádár died three weeks later, on the very day that the
Hungarian Supreme Court announced Imre Nagy's full
legal rehabilitation. Shakespeare would not have risked
such a crude tragic irony. Kádár was buried in the
Kerepesi cemetery, in a 'pantheon of the workers' movement'. Nearby lie the bodies of communists who died
fighting against the insurrection of 1956.

The Hungarian funeral was, like the Polish elections, a
landmark in the post-war history of Eastern Europe. It
clearly marked the end of the post-1956 period which is
inextricably associated with the name of János Kádár.
Kádár died with his time. But of what it marked the
beginning was less clear.

Reactions to the funeral were mixed. Some in the
more radical part of the opposition felt that the Committee for Historical Justice had made too many conces-

sions to the reform communists. Although relatives and friends of Nagy had actually organized the event, it acquired the character almost of a state funeral. Leading Party reformers such as Imre Pozsgay, the prime minister Miklós Németh, and the president of the parliament, Mátyás Szűrös, had been allowed to take their turn at standing guard beside the coffin of Imre Nagy. It almost seemed that the authorities had managed to reclaim the revolution for themselves.

Those who had an unquestionable claim to the legacy of Imre Nagy were less offended. 'Try to be happy with us,' the writer Árpád Göncz gently admonished me. And the most moving experience of all was not the grand ceremony or the internment, but a party at Miklós Vásárhelyi's flat with a small circle of relatives, survivors and friends, some on their first visit to Budapest for more than thirty years. Outwardly, it was just a quiet drinks party. But the deep, inward glow of satisfaction was like nothing, except, perhaps, the feeling of having just voted Solidarity into parliament. They had lived to see the day. And if, politically, it helped Imre Pozsgay to force the pace of reform inside the Party, well, that was all to the good too. For they were less ready than angry Young Democrats to say that even a radically reformed Party had no part to play in the transformation of Hungary. Imre Nagy was, after all, a communist.

An historian friend, by contrast, described the Heroes' Square event as a 'masquerade'. She compared it with the ceremonies of almost a century before, when the hero of 1848, Lajos Kossuth, was buried in state by a regime he abhorred. There was something in this, too. Thus it was curious to watch, for example, the historian and President of the Hungarian Academy of Sciences, Professor Iván T. Berend, prominently paying his respects before the coffins. To be sure, he was a clever man who had tried to get as near the truth as was compatible with making an impressive career within the official Kádárite establishment. He chaired the Party sub-committee which began the official rehabilitation of Nagy. There were many worse. But what would he have said just a few years before to a member of the Academy who proposed to say publicly what everyone was now saying? 'The time is not yet ripe'? Of course the fortunate Westerner is in no position to sit in judgement, for who knows how you or I would behave in such circumstances? But this is no reason to ignore all differences. Historical justice, like treason, is a matter of date:

> Then to side with Truth is noble when we share her wretched crust,
> Ere her cause bring fame and profit, and 'tis prosperous to be just.

The largest questions concerned the response in the country at large. Here some feared—or hoped, according to viewpoint—that the very subdued outward manifestation of popular feeling indicated a deep, sluggish residue of scepticism, apathy and suspicion of all politics. Others said that the longer-term impact of the event, and above all of the nationwide televising of the event, could not be overestimated. It would, they suggested, break through a crucial barrier of fear. And then the emotions and memories that people had inwardly repressed for half a lifetime, would re-emerge with a vengeance. The most optimistic assessment came from the controversial Young Democrat, Viktor Orbán. The funeral of Imre Nagy would be to Hungary, he said, what the first visit of Pope John Paul II had been to Poland. Clear the decks for a Hungarian Solidarity?

In fact, neither the greatest hopes nor the greatest fears were realized. There was no massive social mobilization. Active participation in politics remained largely confined to the intelligentsia. But nor did things simply go the Party reformers' way. To be sure, that was the immediate political result. At a Central Committee plenum one week after the Nagy funeral, they effectively toppled Károly Grósz (hailed by Mrs Thatcher just a year before as a man in her own image), replacing him with a presidium of four, in which he was a minority of one, beside Pozsgay, Németh and the veteran economic reformer, Rezső Nyers. It was then Nyers, not Grósz, who represented Hungary at a Warsaw Pact summit in Bucharest. The plenum also announced the date for an extraordinary Party conference: 7 October. But the story of the next few months was not just that of the battle within the Party. Beside the external struggles fought mainly in the media, and a series of by-elections won by opposition candidates, this was above all the story of immensely complex and Byzantine negotiations between the Party (insofar as you could still talk of one Party) and the very diverse opposition groups.

These negotiations might loosely be compared with the Polish Round Table. But whereas the Polish Party negotiated with Solidarity *at* a Round Table, the Hungarian Party was negotiating *with* a Round Table. The Opposition Round Table was an umbrella organization that brought together the most important opposition parties and groups. It was founded shortly after the 15 March anniversary demonstration, which had shown how effective joint actions could be, and co-ordinated by a small independent group acceptable to all, the Independent Lawyers' Forum. For some time, they argued with the authorities just about the shape of the table.

The authorities wanted a Polish-style round one. The Opposition Round Table, being itself round, wanted a regular two-sided one: us and them. They compromised on a three-sided table, with the third side seating representatives of what in Britain have been called 'quangos'—quasi non-governmental organizations— although in the Hungarian case they should perhaps rather be called 'quapos', that is, quasi non-Party organizations. The talks were chaired by the President of Parliament, Mátyás Szűrös, who sat alone on the fourth side.

They began on 13 June, three days before the Nagy funeral. Opening for the opposition, the lawyer Imre Konya said: 'We must now carry out peacefully the task of three unfulfilled Hungarian revolutions.' By the calendar these talks lasted just over three months, a month longer than Poland's. However that included a month's time out in August, partly because the talks had reached a stalemate, but perhaps also because it was, well, holiday time. As in Poland, for this period the table was effectively the highest political instance in the land.

An agreement was finally signed on 18 September. Like the Polish Round Table agreement this was a complex document, including a series of draft laws and constitutional amendments on issues ranging from election procedures and the status of political parties to changes in the penal code. Unlike the Polish agreement, it envisaged a fully free parliamentary election. Before that free election, however, the president was to be elected by the old, compromised and still largely conformist parliament. Rather as in Poland where there was a nod-and-wink understanding that the job would go to Jaruzelski, so here there was a certain understanding

57

that the job would probably go to Imre Pozsgay. But the most clearly anti-communist opposition groups, the Free Democrats (heirs to the earlier democratic opposition), the Young Democrats, and the Independent Trade Unions, broke that consensus before the ink was dry. These three groups refused to sign the agreement at all.

In order to press their point, the Free Democrats then swiftly organized a street-corner campaign which succeeded in obtaining some 200,000 signatures for a petition requesting a referendum on four issues, of which the most important was the proposal to delay the presidential election until after the free election to parliament. The Party then provided a nice diversion by proposing that the president should be elected not by parliament but by a direct vote, which they believed that Pozsgay would still have a chance of winning. The Free Democrats were having none of that. Yet while the Free Democrats' campaign might at first glance seem to have been directed mainly against the communists, it was in fact almost as much directed against their chief opposition rivals, the Hungarian Democratic Forum. In the course of it, the Free Democrats both boosted their own membership and established their anti-communist credentials with a wider public. Altogether, the opposition parties were somewhat busier fighting each other than they were fighting the communists.

This might seem foolish, when, unlike in Poland, the communists still formed the government. But it was based on a fair estimate of the real power relations in the country. And after 7 October, people could very well ask: 'What communists?' For on the first evening of its congress, the Hungarian Socialist Workers' Party dissolved itself, dropped the Workers, and resumed its deliberations as the Hungarian Socialist Party. This seemed to be a triumph for the reformers. But the old-new party's membership grew only very slowly, reaching little more than 50,000 by the end of the year. Meanwhile a new-old communist party re-emerged, calling itself, defiantly, the Hungarian Socialist Workers' Party, and led by none other than Károly Grósz.

On 18 October the parliament went ahead and passed the constitutional amendments supposedly agreed at the talks with the Opposition Round Table. The most dramatic of these dropped the People from the name of the state, and changed the preamble to the constitution so it now declared that 'the Hungarian Republic is an independent, democratic state based on the rule of law, in which the values of bourgeois democracy and democratic socialism are equally recognized.' (So here socialism did scrape in.)

At noon on 23 October, the thirty-third anniversary of the outbreak of the 1956 revolution, Mátyás Szűrös then formally proclaimed the new Hungarian Republic from the balcony of the magnificent parliament building on the banks of the Danube. He started by saying, to loud applause, that the new constitution was 'motivated by the historic lessons of the historic uprising and national independence movement of October 1956.' But then he made a terrible misjudgement, declaring, 'We continue to regard the undisturbed and balanced development of our relationship with our great neighbour, the Soviet Union, as being in our country's national interest.' True enough, perhaps, but hardly the words for this occasion. The crowd whistled and booed. In the evening, three separate memorial marches met up in front of the parliament, for a genuinely free and independent celebration, with speeches from old men who had served long prison terms, and young men clambering on statues.

Then it was back to politics as usual. The Free Democrats got their referendum, won it by a narrow margin, and therefore had the presidential election postponed until after the free general election, which was scheduled for 25 March 1990. So confusing was the political scene that when pollsters included in one of their surveys the name of a wholly fictitious party, the Hungarian Democratic Party, twelve per cent of those asked said they supported it.

Hungary thus took things in a different order from Poland. In effect, it had multi-party politics before it had democracy. The government was still largely composed of members of the old-new Party. Poland, by contrast, had a largely non-communist government, but limited, popular front, coalition politics. In the months and years ahead the two countries would surely play leap-frog, each trying get ahead of the other and keep the attention of the West. But two things they had in common. In both, the relatively long drawn-out politics of 'refolution' had deepened the economic crisis that was a major factor in precipitating the changes in the first place. But equally, in both the political breakthrough had unmistakeably come. In Hungary, there was perhaps no single moment in 1989 quite so decisive as the election of 4 June in Poland. But for symbolism and emotion, the funeral of 16 June ran it very close.

On the day before the funeral, I met one of the survivors, the wry and charming old Árpád Göncz. 'You know,' he said, 'I'm happy to have lived to see the end of this disaster, but I want to die before the beginning of the next one.' Hungarian pessimism is as incurable as Polish optimism, yet both are as richly endowed with Central Europe's greatest natural resource: irony.

Berlin: Wall's End

Once upon a time, and a very bad time it was, there was a famous platform in West Berlin where distinguished visitors would be taken to stare at the Wall. American Presidents from Kennedy to Reagan stood on that platform looking out over the no man's land beyond. They were told that this, the Potsdamer Platz, had once been Berlin's busiest square, its Piccadilly Circus. Their hosts pointed out a grassy mound on the far side: the remains of Hitler's bunker. East German border-guards watched impassively, or rode up and down the death strip on their army motorbikes.

On the morning of Sunday, 12 November I walked through the Wall and across that no man's land with a crowd of East Berliners, a watchtower to our left, Hitler's bunker to our right. Bewildered border-guards waved us through. (As recently as February their colleagues had shot dead a man trying to escape.) Vertical segments of the wall stood at ease where the crane had just dumped them, their multicoloured graffiti facing east for the first time. A crowd of West Berliners applauded as we came through, and a man handed out free city plans. Then I turned round and walked back again, past more bewildered border-guards and customs officers. Ahead of me I noticed a tall man in an unfamiliar green uniform. He turned out to be the US commandant in Berlin, one General Haddock.

By nightfall, West Berlin workers had dismantled the famous platform, like an unneeded prop. Europe's

Mousetrap had ended its twenty-eight-year run. Clear the stage for another show.

Everyone has seen the pictures of joyful celebration in West Berlin, the vast crowds stopping the traffic on the Kürfurstendamm, *Sekt* corks popping, strangers tearfully embracing—the greatest street-party in the history of the world. Yes, it was like that. But it was not only like that. Most of the estimated two million East Germans who flooded into West Berlin over the weekend simply walked the streets in quiet family groups, often with toddlers in pushchairs. They queued up at a bank to collect the 100 Deutschmarks 'greeting money' (about thirty-five pounds) offered to visiting East Germans by the West German government, and then they went, very cautiously, shopping. Generally they bought one or two small items, perhaps some fresh fruit, a Western newspaper and toys for the children. Then, clasping their carrier-bags, they walked quietly back through the Wall, through the grey, deserted streets of East Berlin, home.

It is very difficult to describe the quality of this experience because what they actually did was so stunningly ordinary. In effect, they just took a bus from Hackney or Dagenham to Piccadilly Circus, and went shopping in the West End. Berliners walked the streets of Berlin. What could be more normal? And yet, what could be more fantastic! 'Twenty-eight years and ninety-one days,' says one man in his late thirties strolling back up Friedrichstrasse. Twenty-eight years and ninety-one days since the building of the Wall. On that day, in August 1961, his parents had wanted to go to a late-night Western in a West Berlin cinema, but their eleven-year-old son had been too tired. In the early hours they woke to the sound of tanks. He had never been to West Berlin from that day to this. A taxi-driver asks me, with a sly smile: 'How much is the ferry to England?' The day before yesterday his question would have been unthinkable.

Everyone, but everyone, on the streets of East Berlin has just been, or is just going to West Berlin. A breathless, denim-jacketed couple stop me to ask, 'Is this the way out?' They have come hot-foot from Leipzig. 'Our hearts are going pitter-pat,' they say, in broad Saxon dialect. Everyone looks the same as they make their way home—except for the tell-tale Western carrier-bag. But everyone is inwardly changed, changed utterly. 'Now people are standing up straight,' says a hotel porter. 'They are speaking their minds. Even work is more fun. I think the sick will get up from their hospital beds.' And it was in East rather than West Berlin that this weekend had the magic, pentecostal quality which I last experienced in Poland in autumn 1980. Ordinary men and women find their voice and their courage— *Lebensmut*, as the porter puts it. These are moments when you feel that somewhere an angel has opened his wings.

They may have been ordinary people doing very ordinary things, but the Berliners immediately grasped the historical dimensions of the event. 'Of course the real villain was Hitler,' said one. A note stuck to a remnant of the Wall read: 'Stalin is dead, Europe lives.' The man who counted twenty-eight years and ninety-one days told me he had been most moved by an improvised poster saying: 'Only today is the war really over.'

Bild newspaper—West Germany's *Sun*—carried a black-red-gold banner headline declaring 'Good Morning, Germany', and underneath it an effusive thank-you letter from the editors to Mikhail Gorbachev. The East Germans also felt grateful to Gorbachev. But more important, they felt they had won this opening for themselves. For it was only the pressure of their massive, peaceful demonstrations that compelled the Party leadership to take this step. 'You see, it shows Lenin was wrong,' observed one worker. 'Lenin said a revolution could succeed only with violence. But this was a peaceful revolution.' And even the Party's Central Committee acknowledged at the beginning of its hastily drafted Action Programme that 'a revolutionary people's movement has set in motion a process of profound upheavals.'

Why did it happen? And why so quickly? No one in East Germany predicted it. To be sure in July, when I was finally allowed back by the GDR authorities, after applying in vain for several years, officials would say that the situation was *sehr kompliziert*, and shake their heads. But Church and opposition activists remained deeply pessimistic. The State Security Service—the 'Stasi'—still seemed all-powerful, the population at large not prepared to risk its modest prosperity. Above all, the ranks of the opposition had been continuously thinned by emigration to West Germany. For taking part in a demonstration, a young man would be threatened with a long prison term; then he would be taken into another room of the police station where another officer would present him with a neatly completed application to emigrate. Prison or the West. As one friend put it: 'It's like being asked to choose between heaven and hell.' 'Soon,' he added bitterly, 'there'll be nobody left in this country but a mass of stupid philistines and a few crazy idealists.'

With hindsight we may be a little wiser. At the very least, one can list in order some factors that brought the cup of popular discontent to overflowing. In the beginning was the Wall itself: the Wall and the system it both represented and preserved. The Wall was not round the periphery of East Germany, it was at its very centre. And it ran through every heart. It was difficult even for people from other East European countries to appreciate the full psychological burden it imposed. An East Berlin doctor wrote a book describing the real sicknesses—and of course the suicides—that resulted. He called it *The Wall Sickness*. In a sense, the mystery was always why the people of East Germany did not revolt.

The second causal factor, both in time and importance, was Gorbachev. The 'Gorbachev effect' was strongest in East Germany because it was more strongly oriented towards—and ultimately dependent on—the Soviet Union than any other East European state. It was not for nothing that a 1974 amendment to the constitution proclaimed: 'The German Democratic Republic is for ever and irrevocably allied with the Union of Soviet Socialist Republics.' East Germany's young people had for years been told, *Von der Sowjetunion lernen heisst siegen lernen*—'To learn from the Soviet Union is to learn how to win.' So they did! For several years East Germans had been turning the name of Gorbachev, and the Soviet example, against their rulers. And Gorbachev personally gave the last push—on his visit to join the fortieth-anniversary celebrations of the GDR on 7 October—with his carefully calculated utterance that 'Life itself punishes those who delay', the leaked news that he had told Honecker Soviet troops would not be used for internal repression and (according to well-informed West German sources) his direct encouragement to the likes of Egon Krenz and the Berlin Party chief Günter Schabowski, to move to depose Honecker.

The Polish and Hungarian examples were not so important. To be sure, everyone learned about them, in great detail, from the West German television they watched nightly. To be sure, developments in those two countries demonstrated that fundamental changes were possible. But for most people the economic misery in Poland more than cancelled out the political example. Hungary—a favoured holiday destination for East Germans, with a better economic situation and a history (and, dare one say, national character) less fatefully at odds with Germany's—Hungary perhaps had a greater impact. Yet the crucial Hungarian input was not the example of its internal reforms, but the opening of its frontier with Austria.

As soon as the Hungarians starting cutting the barbed wire of the 'iron curtain', in May, East Germans began to escape across it. As the numbers grew, and East Germans gathered in refugee camps in Budapest, the Hungarian authorities decided, in early September, to let them leave officially (suspending a bilateral consular agreement with the GDR). The trickle turned into a flood: some 15,000 crossed the border in the first three days, 50,000 by the end of October. Others sought an exit route via the West German embassies in Prague and Warsaw. This was the final catalyst for internal change in East Germany.

Church-protected opposition activity had been increasing through the summer. There had been independent monitoring of the local elections in May, which clearly showed that they were rigged. In June, the East German authorities' emphatic endorsement of the repression in China brought another round of protests. It is important to recall that right up to, and during, the fortieth-anniversary celebrations on 7 October, the police used force, indeed gratuitous brutality, to disperse these protests and intimidate any who might have contemplated joining in. Young men were dragged along the cobbled streets by their hair. Women and children were thrown into prison. Innocent bystanders were beaten.

If one can identify a turning-point it was perhaps Monday, 9 October, the day after Gorbachev left. Since the late summer, the regular Monday evening 'prayers for peace' in Leipzig's Church of St Nicholas had been followed by small demonstrations on the adjacent Karl-Marx-Platz. At the outset, most of the demonstrators were people who wanted to emigrate. But on 25 September there were between 5,000 and 8,000 people, with the would-be emigrants now in a minority, and on 2 October, as the emigration crisis deepened, there were perhaps 15,000 to 20,000—the largest spontaneous demonstration in East Germany since the uprising of 17 June 1953. They sung the Internationale and demanded the legalization of the recently founded 'citizens' initiative', New Forum. The police were baffled, and in places peacefully overwhelmed.

On Monday, 9 October, however, following the violent repression during the fortieth anniversary celebrations two days earlier, riot police, army units, and factory 'combat groups' stood ready to clear the Karl-Marx-Platz, East Germany's Tiananmen Square. An article in the local paper by the commander of one of these 'combat groups' said they were prepared to defend socialism 'if need be, with weapon in hand.' But in the event some 70,000 people came out to make their peaceful protest, and this time force was not used to disperse them. (The figure of 70,000, like all the other crowd figures, can only be taken as a very crude estimate, at best an order of magnitude.) It was claimed, by sources close to the new party leader Egon Krenz, that he, being in overall political control of internal security, had taken the brave, Gorbachevian decision not to use force. It was even claimed that he had personally gone to Leipzig to prevent bloodshed.

Subsequent accounts by those actually involved in Leipzig gave a quite different picture. By these accounts, the crucial action was taken by the famous Leipzig conductor, Kurt Masur, together with a well-known cabaret artist, Bernd-Lutz Lange, and a priest, Peter Zimmermann. They managed to persuade three local Party leaders to join them in a dramatic, last-minute appeal for non-violence, which was read in the churches, broadcast over loudspeakers—and relayed to the police by the acting Party chief in Leipzig. This made the difference between triumph and disaster. It was, it seems, only later in the evening that Krenz telephoned to ask what was happening. The moment was, none the less, decisive for Krenz's bid for power. Nine days later he replaced Honecker as Party leader. But in those nine days the revolution had begun.

To say the growth of popular protest was exponential would be an understatement. It was a non-violent explosion. Those extraordinary, peaceful, determined Monday evening demonstrations in Leipzig—always starting with 'peace prayers' in the churches—grew week-by-week, from 70,000 to double that, to 300,000, to perhaps half a million. The whole of East Germany suddenly went into labour, an old world—to recall Marx's image—pregnant with the new. From that time forward the people acted and the Party reacted. 'Freedom!' demanded the Leipzig demonstrators, and Krenz announced a new travel law. 'Free travel!' said the crowds, and Krenz reopened the frontier to Hungary. 'A suggestion for May Day: let the leadership parade past the people,' said a banner, quoted by the writer Christa Wolf in the massive, peaceful demonstration in East Berlin on 4 November. And more leaders stepped down. 'Free elections!' demanded the people, and the Council of Ministers resigned *en masse*. 'We are the people!' they chanted, and the party leadership opened the Wall.

The cup of bitterness was already full to the brim. The years of Wall Sickness, the lies, the stagnation, the Soviet and Hungarian examples, the rigged elections, the police violence—all added their dose. The instant that repression was lifted, the cup flowed over. And then, with amazing speed, the East Germans discovered what the Poles had discovered ten years earlier, during the Pope's visit in 1979. They discovered their solidarity. 'Long live the October Revolution of 1989' proclaimed another banner on the Alexanderplatz. And so it was: the first peaceful revolution in German history.

Yet the opening of the Berlin Wall on 9 November, and subsequently of the whole inter-German frontier, changed the terms of the revolution completely. Before 9 November, the issue had been how this state—the German Democratic Republic—should be governed. The people were reclaiming their so-called people's state. They were putting the D for Democratic into the GDR. After 9 November, the issue was whether this state should continue to exist at all.

I witnessed this moment of change at the epicentre of the revolution, in Leipzig, on a bitterly cold Monday evening twelve days after the opening of the Wall. Driving down the 1930s autobahn from Berlin, I listened on the car radio to a discussion with a local leader of the newly formed Social Democratic Party (SDP). What are your basic principles? he was asked. He went on rather vaguely about the lower social strata being able to emancipate themselves, but not oppressing others in their turn, as the communists had. 'So,' said the interviewer, 'you don't want a dictatorship?' 'No, we don't want a dictatorship.' Very reassuring. Then there was a sulphur dioxide level warning for the Leipzig area.

Through freezing mist (or smog?) I found my way to the packed Church of St Nicholas. Inside, the homily was about Cain and Abel. People like Cain should not be allowed to carry on in power, said the preacher. But they should have the chance to live on, to make amends. The theme of the whole service was the need for understanding, tolerance, reconciliation. Yet there was not too much of that spirit on display in the vast crowd outside, on and around Karl-Marx-Platz. Placards showed Erich Honecker in prison uniform and behind bars. Speaker after speaker denounced forty years of lies, corruption, privilege and waste.

A source of palpable fascination was the rulers' alleged abuse of hard-currency transfers from West Germany. 'Where has all the hard currency gone?' people sang, to the tune of 'Where have all the flowers gone?' And one speaker answered, to rapturous applause, with fantastic tales of how the Party leaders had bought themselves a whole island in the Caribbean, and how Margot Honecker, the former education minister and wife of Erich Honecker, used to fly to Paris every month for a hair-do. Other speakers demanded that the mass youth organization, the so-called Free German Youth, should be dissolved, and that the Party should (as in Hungary) get out of the workplace. Everyone agreed on two immediate central demands: free elections and an end to the Party's *Führungsanspruch*— its 'leadership claim'.

But that was only half the story. The other half was given most eloquently by someone who introduced himself as 'a plain craftsman'. 'Socialism has not delivered what it promised,' he said, and the promised 'new socialism' would not deliver it either. Loud applause. 'We are not laboratory rabbits.' They had waited and laboured long enough. They all knew that a free-market economy works. 'Our compatriots in the Federal Republic are not foreigners.' There should therefore, he said, be a referendum on reunification. At this point a small group started chanting the slogan that was already painted on several banners: *'Deutschland, einig Vaterland!'* 'Germany, united fatherland!' (words from the East German 'national' anthem on account of which the Honecker leadership had ordered that the whole anthem should never be sung, only the music played). The vast crowd quickly took up the chant: *'Deutschland, einig Vaterland!'* they roared, 'DEUTSCHLAND, EINIG VATERLAND!' And I had to pinch myself to make sure that I was not dreaming, that I really was standing on Karl-Marx-Platz, in Leipzig, in the middle of East Germany, while a hundred thousand voices cried, 'Germany, united fatherland!'

In this crowd, it must be said, almost every conceivable tendency (except communism) was represented. Green banners were raised behind those demanding reunification, a placard saying 'Free Farmers' beside a blue-and-gold European Community flag. Yet one

71

already felt, instinctively, that the voices for reunification were the voices that would prevail. Not because of the power of nationalism. Just because of the power of common sense. The alternatives offered by the fledgling opposition groups, whether New Forum, the SDP, 'Democratic Awakening' or 'Democracy Now', were so vague, inchoate, uncertain. The alternative offered by West Germany was just so immediately, so obviously, so overwhelmingly plausible. 'Mercedes! Buy the *Sachsenring* factory!' demanded another banner at the front of the crowd. The frontiers were open. The people had seen West Germany—and it worked.

On the subsequent march around the city's ring boulevard I noticed one elderly man with a home-made hardboard placard on a stick. It carried the slogan of East Germany's October revolution: *'Wir sind das Volk.'* But the *das* was crossed out and replaced by *EIN*, so it now read not 'We are the people' but 'We are one nation'. And *'Wir sind EIN Volk'* increasingly supplanted *'Wir sind das Volk'* in the mouths of the people. That the majority in East Germany should long resist the temptation of getting closer together with West Germany seemed as likely as that the East German Mark should long survive free competition with the West German Mark. Indeed the two were intimately related: the currency question and the national question. For most things that ordinary people wanted did depend, sooner or later, on the possession of a hard, convertible currency. (That DM100 'greeting money' was soon spent.) Another banner I spotted on the march round the Ring declared: 'For a convertible currency ... Confederation BRDDR' (that is, Federal Republic [of] German[y] Democratic Republic). The big D was no longer for Democratic. The big D was for *Deutschland*—and Deutschmark. I asked the man holding this banner which party he would vote for in a free election. He replied: 'Certainly not my own ... ' He was a member of the Socialist Unity Party.

This turn of events—or rather of popular aspirations— left the Church and opposition activists who had led the October revolution curiously disconcerted. For their starting-point had always been that they did not want reunification. Rather, they wanted to work for a better, a genuinely democratic German Democratic Republic. They did not regard the Federal Republic as the best of all possible Germanies. They thought there were some achievements and values in the GDR worth preserving: less inequality and exploitation than in West Germany, a greater human solidarity, a more caring attitude, elements of something they still wished to call 'social-ism'. Ideologically, the opposition in the GDR was a curious mixture of Marxist revisionism, social demo-cracy, Green and Peace Movement concerns, and left-wing protestantism—since the late 1960s the Protestant Churches in the GDR had described themselves as a 'church in socialism'. As the Protestant priest Edelbert Richter put it, speaking on behalf of the group called Democratic Awakening: 'Not only the word "socialist" but certain social principles of socialism still sound good to us.' To them—but to the people?

These idealists' reluctance to see East Germany simply disappear into a larger Federal Republic—to 'sell out' as they would put it—was not, however, fully explicable in terms of reason and ideology. Emotion and personal history had as much to do with it. Every one of these men and women had at some point confronted the decision whether to leave for the West, as so many of their friends and colleagues had done—to make, as it

73

were, an individual reunification. They had decided to stay, to go on working inside the country for a better GDR, a better Germany. A close friend of mine, a pastor, actually *returned* to East Germany after the building of the Wall. 'People will need me here,' he said. And they certainly did.

Were they now at once to concede that it had all been in vain? 'I don't want to say these forty years have just been wasted,' observed Bärbel Bohley, an artist and leading figure in the New Forum, 'because in that case I might as well have left twenty years ago.' Already in January 1990 they began to look back to the month from 9 October to 9 November as an irretrievable moment, a brief flowering of civic courage, peaceful maturity and social self-organization that was blighted not by a cold wind from the East, but by the warm, perfumed wind from the West. For it was at once East Germany's chance and its tragedy that, unlike in Poland or Hungary, the boundaries of social self-determination and national self-determination were not the same.

By the end of 1989, the desperately confused and volatile politics of East Germany were therefore quite unlike those of its neighbours. To be sure, here, too, there was a Round Table; indeed there were countless round tables, national, regional and local. At these round tables, those who still wanted to make a better GDR tried to find common ground with those who still held the tattered remnants of power, and to explain to them why they must yield even those. In East Germany, as in Poland and Hungary, the Round Table briefly became the highest instance in the land. Here, too, they at once set a date for free elections, and the pseudo-parliament voted to remove from the constitution all reference to the leading role of the Party. Here, too, the membership and power of that Party evaporated at quite breathtaking speed, taking with it the most formidable security apparatus in Europe—the dreaded 'Stasi'. (Unforgettable was the sight of the head of that ministry, General Erich Mielke, retreating from the microphone at the People's Chamber mumbling, *'Aber ich liebe Euch doch alle!'*—'But I love you all!') Here, even more than elsewhere, the remaining Communist leaders helped by their own blunders to hasten their own demise: notably by an extraordinarily misjudged attempt to reintroduce a State Security Service, supposedly to protect people against far right or 'neo-Nazi' groups. But there, at the latest, the similarities end.

For the overwhelming fact of East German political life at the beginning of 1990 was the flood-tide towards a re- or rather new-unification with West Germany. This took several forms. There were the demands on the streets, and in all political meetings, to which every opposition group had to adapt—or face obliteration at the polls. (Symptomatically, the Social Democratic Party—SDP—renamed itself, like its illustrious forebear, and like the West German party, *Sozialdemokratische Partei Deutschlands*, SPD. Again, the big D for Democratic became the big D for *Deutschland*.) There was the growing number of people who simply voted for reunification with their feet, by emigrating to West Germany: some 2,000 a day in January 1990, the same number that had originally precipitated the building of the Wall in August 1961. And then there were innumerable examples of practical co-operation and joint enterprise across the inter-German frontier and through the Wall: new air links, bus routes, joint ventures.

This was most dramatically visible in Berlin. Where

previously a West Berlin underground line ran through ghostly, sealed underground stations in East Berlin, the doors of the train now opened and East Berliners leapt aboard. The whole mental geography of Berlin changed overnight. What had been the edge became the centre. It was one city again. But it was also true all around the German-German borders. Unification was happening from below. It happened because many people on both sides wanted it to happen. Just how many people, and on what conditions, only the elections of 1990—in East and West—would show.

If there were uncertainties about the post-revolutionary transitions in Poland and Hungary they were nothing compared to those in East Germany, no, in Germany as a whole. The West German government, which for decades had urged the East German regime to let the people go, was now delighted but also appalled by the consequences of the regime doing precisely that. For the people were coming to West Germany at a rate which threatened to overwhelm their housing market and welfare state, and, above all, to provoke a domestic political backlash. Unless the Bonn government was prepared to build a Wall of its own, the only way to prevent more and more East Germans coming West seemed to be to offer a perspective of, at the very least, rapid economic unification. Big D for Deutschmark. But how could this be done? And if economic and monetary union led to political union in mid-nineteenth-century Germany, and was meant to do so in late-twentieth-century Western Europe, why in heaven's name should it not do so in late-twentieth-century Germany? But in that case, what about the Soviet troops in East Germany?

To raise these questions here is unwise, for by the time you read this the answers will be clearer. Yet just because as I write, in January 1990, the euphoria of October and November has already turned into consternation and alarm—both in Germany and among her partners and neighbours, to East and West—it seems all the more important to recall that original moment of hope and joy. The moment when people who for years had been silenced could at last speak their minds; when people were free at last to travel, who for years had been locked in. It was a moment of emancipation and liberation, created by the people of East Germany for the people of East Germany. They had waited as long as the other peoples of East Central Europe for this moment, and they had as much right to it as any other people.

Prague: Inside the Magic Lantern

My contribution to the velvet revolution was a quip. Arriving in Prague on Day Seven (23 November), when the pace of change was already breath-taking, I met Václav Havel in the back-room of his favoured basement pub. I said: 'In Poland it took ten years, in Hungary ten months, in East Germany ten weeks: perhaps in Czechoslovakia it will take ten days!' Grasping my hands, and fixing me with his winning smile, Havel immediately summoned over a video-camera team from the samizdat *Videojournál*, who just happened to be waiting in the corner. I was politely compelled to repeat my quip to camera, over a glass of beer, and then Havel gave his reaction: 'It would be fabulous, if it could be so...' Revolution, he said, is too exhausting.

The camera team dashed off to copy the tape, so that it could be shown on television sets in public places. Havel subsequently used the conceit in several interviews. And because he used it, it made a fantastic career. It was repeated in the Czechoslovak papers. An opposition spokesman recalled it in a television broadcast just before the general strike—on Day Eleven. It was on the front page of the Polish opposition daily, *Gazeta Wyborcza*. It surfaced in the Western press. And when I finally had to leave Prague on Day Nineteen, with the revolution by no means over, people were still saying: 'You see, with us—ten days!' Such is the magic of round numbers.

I tell this story not just from author's vanity, but also because it illustrates several qualities of the most delightful of all the year's Central European revolutions: the speed, the improvisation, the merriness, and the absolutely central role of Václav Havel, who was at once director, playwright, stage-manager and leading actor in this, his greatest play. I was only one of many—indeed of millions—to feed him some lines.

Next morning I received a complimentary theatre ticket. A ticket to the Magic Lantern Theatre, whose subterranean stage, auditorium, foyers and dressing-rooms had become the headquarters of the main opposition coalition in the Czech lands, the Civic Forum, and thus, in effect, the headquarters of the revolution. The ticket changed. At first it was just a small notelet with the words 'Please let in and out' written in purple ink, signed by Václav Havel's brother, Ivan, and authenticated by the playwright's rubber stamp. This shows a beaming pussy cat with the word 'Smile!' across his chest. Then it was a green card worn around the neck, with my name typed as 'Timothy Gordon Ash', and the smiling cat again. Then it was a xeroxed and initialled paper slip saying 'Civic Forum building', this time with two smiling cats (one red, one black) and a beaming green frog. I have it in front of me as I write. Beneath the frog it says 'très bien'.

In any case, the tickets worked wonders. For nearly two weeks I, as an historian, was privileged to watch history being made inside the Magic Lantern. For most of that time, I was the only foreigner to sit in on the hectic deliberations of what most people called simply 'the Forum'. But before describing what I saw, we must briefly rehearse the first act.

Students started it. Small groups of them had been active for at least a year. They edited faculty magazines.

They organized discussion clubs. They worked on the borderline between official and unofficial life. Many had contacts with the opposition, all read samizdat. Some say they had formed a conspiratorial group called 'The Ribbon'—the Czech 'White Rose'. But they also worked through the official youth organization, the SSM. It was through the SSM that they got permission to hold a demonstration in Prague on 17 November, to mark the fiftieth anniversary of the martyrdom of Jan Opletal, a Czech student murdered by the Nazis. This began, as officially scheduled, in Prague's second district, with speeches and tributes at the cemetery.

But the numbers grew, and the chants turned increasingly against the present dictators in the castle. The demonstrators decided—perhaps some had planned all along—to march to Wenceslas Square, the stage for all the historic moments of Czech history, whether in 1918, 1948, or 1968. Down the hill they went, along the embankment of the River Vltava, and then, turning right at the National Theatre, up Narodní avenue into the square. Here they were met by riot police, with white helmets, shields and truncheons, and by special anti-terrorist squads, in red berets. Large groups were cut off and surrounded, both along Narodní and in the square. They went on chanting 'Freedom' and singing the Czech version of 'We Shall Overcome'. Those in the front line tried to hand flowers to the police. They placed lighted candles on the ground and raised their arms, chanting, 'We have bare hands.' But the police, and especially the red-berets, beat men, women and children with their truncheons.

This was the spark that set Czechoslovakia alight. During the night from Friday to Saturday—with reports of one dead and many certainly in hospital—some students determined to go on strike. On Saturday morning they managed to spread the word to most of the Charles University, and to several other institutions of higher learning, which immediately joined the occupation strike. (Patient research will be needed to reconstruct the precise details of this crucial moment.) On Saturday afternoon they were joined by actors, already politicized by earlier petitions in defence of Václav Havel, and drawn in directly by the very active students from the drama and film academies. They met in the Realistic Theatre. Students described the 'massacre', as it was now called. The theatre people responded with a declaration of support which not only brought the theatres out on strike—that is, turned their auditoria into political debating chambers—but also, and, so far as I could establish, for the first time, made the proposal for a general strike on Monday, 27 November, between noon and two p.m. The audience responded with a standing ovation.

On Sunday morning the students of the film and drama academies came out with an appropriately dramatic declaration. Entitled 'Don't wait—Act!', it began by saying that 1989 in Czechoslovakia might sadly be proclaimed the 'year of the truncheon'. 'That truncheon,' it continued, ' on Friday, 17 November spilled the blood of students.' And then, after appealing 'especially to European states in the year of the two hundredth anniversary of the French revolution', they went on to list demands which ranged from the legal registration of the underground monthly *Lidové Noviny* to removing the leading role of the communist party from the constitution, but also crucially repeated the call for the general strike. (Within a few days the students had all their proclamations neatly stored in personal computers, and many of the flysheets on the streets were actually computer print-outs.)

It was only at ten o'clock on Sunday evening (Day Three), after the students and actors had taken the lead, proclaiming both their own and the general strike, that the previously existing opposition groups, led by Charter 77, met in another Prague theatre. The effective convener of this meeting was Václav Havel, who had hurried back from his farmhouse in Northern Bohemia when he heard news of the 'massacre'. The meeting included not only the very diverse opposition groups, such as the Committee for the Defence of the Unjustly Prosecuted (VONS), the Movement for Civic Freedoms and *Obroda* (Rebirth), the club of excommunicated communists, but also individual members of the previously puppet People's and Socialist Parties. The latter was represented by its general secretary, one Jan Škoda, who was once a schoolmate and close friend of Václav Havel's, but had carefully avoided him through the long, dark years of so-called normalization.

This miscellaneous late-night gathering agreed to establish an *Občanské Fórum*, a Civic Forum, 'as a spokesman on behalf of that part of the Czechoslovak public which is increasingly critical of the existing Czechoslovak leadership and which in recent days has been profoundly shaken by the brutal massacre of peacefully demonstrating students.' It made four demands: the immediate resignation of the communist leaders responsible for preparing the Warsaw Pact intervention in 1968 and the subsequent devastation of the country's life, starting with the president, Gustáv Husák, and the Party leader, Miloš Jakeš; the immediate resignation of the federal interior minister, František Kincl, and the Prague first secretary, Miroslav Štěpán, held responsible for violent repression of peaceful demonstrations; the establishment of a special commission to investigate these police actions; and the immediate release of all prisoners of conscience. The Civic Forum, it added, supports the call for a general strike. From this time forward, the Forum assumed the leadership of the revolution in the Czech lands. (In Slovakia there sprung up a different organization with a different name: The Public Against Violence.)

Over this weekend there had been tens of thousands of people, mainly young people, milling around on Wenceslas Square, waving flags and chanting slogans. Students had taken over the equestrian statue of the good king, at the top of his square, covering its base with improvised posters, photographs and candles. But the popular breakthrough came on Monday afternoon. For now the square was not merely teeming; it was packed. Dense masses chanted 'Freedom', 'Resign', and, most strikingly, a phrase that might be translated as 'Now's the time' or 'This is it'. And neither the white helmets nor the red berets moved in. As in East Germany, when the authorities woke up to what was happening, it was already too late. (But the then prime minister, Ladislav Adamec, went out of his way to emphasize that martial law would not be declared, thus implying that the option had been considered.)

On Tuesday, Day Five, the demonstration—at four p.m., after working hours—was even larger. The publishing house of the Socialist Party, under Jan Škoda, made available its balcony, perfectly located half-way down the square. From here the veteran Catholic opposition activist, Radim Palouš, a dynamic banned priest, Václav Malý, and then Havel addressed the vast crowd, repeating the Forum's demands. Next morning the first edition of the communist party daily *Rudé Právo* had a headline referring to a demonstration of '200,000' in the square. The second edition said '100,000'. Someone made a collage of the two editions, xeroxed it and stuck it up on shop windows, next to the photographs of the pre-war President-Liberator, Tomáš Garrigue Masaryk, the cyclostyled or computer-printed flysheets and the carefully typed declarations that this or that shop would join in the general strike, declarations signed by all the employees and often authenticated with a seal or rubber stamp.

On Wednesday and Thursday, Days Six and Seven, there were yet larger demonstrations, while first talks were held between Prime Minister Adamec and a Forum delegation, which, however, at the prime minister's earnest request, was not led by Václav Havel. The prime minister, Havel told me, sent word via an aide that he did not yet want to 'play his trump card'. At the same time, however, Havel had direct communication with Adamec via a self-constituted group of mediators, calling itself 'the bridge'. 'The bridge' had two struts: Michal Horáček, a journalist on a youth paper, and Michael Kocáb, a rock singer.

The revolution was thus well under way, indeed rocking round the clock. And its headquarters was a just a hundred yards from the bottom of Wenceslas Square, in that theatre called the Magic Lantern.

Through the heavy metal-and-glass doors, past the second line of volunteer guards, you plunge down a broad flight of stairs into a curving, 1950s-style, mirror-lined foyer. People dart around importantly, or sit in little groups on benches, eating improvised canapés and discussing the future of the nation. Down another flight of stairs there is the actual theatre. The set—for Dürrenmatt's *Minotaurus*—is like a funnel, with a hole at the back of the stage just big enough for a small monster to squeeze through. Here, in place of the Magic Lantern's special combination of drama, music and pantomime, they hold the daily press conference: the speakers emerging from the hole designed for Dürrenmatt's monster. Journalists instead of tourists are let in for the performance.

At one end of the foyer there is a room with a glass wall on which it says, in several languages, 'smoking room'. There is another guard at the door. Some are allowed in. Others not. Flash your magic ticket. In. Familiar bearded faces, old friends from the underground, sit around on rickety chairs, in a crisis meeting. A television mounted high on the wall shows an operetta, without the sound. The room smells of cigarette smoke, sweat, damp coats and revolution. I remember the same smell, precisely, from Poland in autumn 1980.

This, you think, is the real headquarters. But after a few hours you discover a black door at the other end of the foyer. Through the door you go down a metal stairway into a narrow, desperately overheated corridor, as if into the bowels of an ocean liner. Here, in dressing-rooms ten and eleven, is the very heart, of the revolution. For here sits Václav Havel, with his 'private secretary' and the few key activists from the Forum who are thrashing out the texts of the latest communiqué, programmatic statement or negotiating position.

In front of the dressing-room door stands a wiry, bearded man in a combat jacket, with his thinning hair knotted at the back, hippy fashion. This is John Bok, a friend of Havel's now in charge of the personal bodyguard, composed mainly of students. During the war,

John Bok's father was a Czech pilot in the Royal Air Force, and the spirit lives. Don't try to mix it with John Bok. He, and Havel's other personal security chief, Stanislav Milota, a former cameraman married to a famous actress, are highly visible characters throughout the performance, surrounding Havel as he dashes around in clouds of nervous flurry, John Bok barking into his walkie-talkie, Milota forever saying 'SHUSH, SHUSH!' in a stage-whisper somewhat louder than the original interruption. In every hectic move, they confirm the playwright's unique status.

A political scientist would be hard pressed to find a term to describe the Forum's structure of decision-making, let alone the hierarchy of authority within it. Yet the structure and hierarchy certainly exist, like a chemist's instant crystals. The 'four-day-old baby', as Havel calls it, is, at first glance, rather like a club. Individual membership is acquired by personal recommendation. You could draw a tree diagram starting from the inaugural meeting in the appropriately named Players' Club Theatre: X introduced Y who introduced Z. The majority of those present have been active in opposition before, the biggest single group being signatories of Charter 77. Twenty years ago they were journalists, academics, politicians, lawyers, but now they come here from their jobs as stokers, window-cleaners, clerks or, at best, banned writers. Sometimes they have to leave a meeting to go and stoke up their boilers. A few of them come straight from prison, whence they have been released under the pressure of popular protest. Politically, they range from the neo-Trotskyist Petr Uhl to the deeply conservative Catholic Václav Benda.

In addition, there are representatives of significant

groups. There are The Students, brightly dressed, radical and politely deferred to by their elders. After all, they started it. Occasionally there are The Actors—although we are all actors now. Then there are The Workers, mainly represented by Petr Miller, an athletic and decisive technician from Prague's huge ČKD engineering combine. All intellectual voices are stilled when The Worker rises to speak. Sometimes there are The Slovaks—demonstratively honoured guests. And then there are those whom I christened The Prognostics, that is, members of the Institute for Forecasting (*Prognostický Ústav*) of the Czechoslovak Academy of Sciences, one of the very few genuinely independent institutes in the whole of the country's official academic life.

The Prognostics are, in fact, economists. Their particular mystique comes from knowing, or believing they know, or, at least, being believed to know, what to do about the economy—a subject clearly high in the minds of the people on the streets, and one on which most of the philosophers, poets, actors, historians assembled here have slightly less expertise than the ordinary worker on the Vysočany tram. The Prognostics are not, of course, unanimous. Dr Václav Klaus, a silver-grey-haired man with glinting metal spectacles, as arrogant as he is clever, favours the solutions of Milton Friedman. His more modest colleague, Dr Tomáš Ježek, is a disciple (and translator) of Friedrich von Hayek.

All these tendencies and groups are represented in the full meetings of the Forum which move, as the numbers grow from tens to hundreds, out of the smoking room into the main auditorium. This 'plenum'—like Solidarity in Poland, the Forum finds itself inadvertently adopting the communist terminology of the last

forty years—then appoints a series of 'commissions'. By
the time I arrive there are, so far as I can gather, four:
Organizational, Technical, Informational and Concep-
tional—the last 'to handle the political science aspect',
as one Forum spokesperson/interpreter rather quaintly
puts it. By the time I leave there seem to be about ten,
each with its 'in-tray'—a white cardboard box lying on
the foyer floor. For example, in addition to 'Concep-
tional' there is also 'Programmatic' and 'Strategic'.

As well as voting people on to these commissions, the
plenum also sometimes selects *ad hoc* 'crisis staffs' and
the groups or individuals to speak on television, negotiate with the government or whatever. When I say
'voting', what actually happens is that the chairman
chooses some names, and then others propose other
names—or themselves. There is no vote. The lists are,
so to speak, open, and therefore long. 'For the Concep-
tional commission I propose Ivan Klíma,' says Havel,
adding: 'Ivan, you don't want to write any more novels,
do you?' Generally the principle of selection is crudely
representative: there must be The Student, The
Worker, The Prognostic etc. Sometimes this produces
marvellous moments to a Western ear. 'Shouldn't we
have a liberal?' says someone, in discussing the Concep-
tional. 'But we've already got two Catholics!' comes the
reply. Thus Catholic means liberal—which here actually means conservative.

To watch all this was to watch politics in a primary,
spontaneous, I almost said 'pure' form. All men and
women may be political animals, but some are more
political than others. It was fascinating to see individuals responding instantly to the scent that wafted
down into the Magic Lantern as the days went by. The
scent of power. People who had never before been

politically active suddenly sat up, edged their way on stage, proposed themselves for a television slot: and you could already see them in a government minister's chair. Others, long active in the democratic opposition, remained seated in the stalls. Not for them the real politics of power.

Like Solidarity, the Forum was racked from the very outset by a conflict between the political imperative of rapid, decisive, united action, and the moral imperative of internal democracy. Should they start as they intended to go on, that is, democratically? Or did the conditions of struggle with a still totalitarian power demand that they should say, to paraphrase Brecht:

> *we who fight for democracy*
> *cannot ourselves be democratic.*

On the face of it, the Forum was, after all, hardly democratic. Who chose them? They chose themselves. Yet already on the second day of their existence they wrote, in a letter addressed to Presidents Bush and Gorbachev, that the Civic Forum 'feels capable of acting as a spokesman for the Czechoslovak public.' By what right? Why, by right of acclamation. For the people were going out on the streets day after day and chanting 'Long live the Forum!' In Prague at least, the people— the *demos*—were obviously, unmistakeably behind them. In this original sense, the Forum was profoundly, elementally democratic. The *demos* spoke, in demos, and declared the Forum to be its mouthpiece.

If one had to describe Havel's leadership, Max Weber's overused term 'charismatic' might for once be apt. It was extraordinary the degree to which everything ultimately revolved around this one man. In almost all the Forum's major decisions and statements he was the final arbiter, the one person who could somehow balance the very different tendencies and interests in the movement. In this sense, many decisions were not made democratically: as in Solidarity. Yet a less authoritarian personality than Havel it would be hard to imagine. (The contrast with Lech Wałęsa was striking.) And the meetings of the plenum were almost absurdly democratic. The avuncular Radim Palouš was an exemplary chairman. Everyone had his or her say. Important issues were decided by vote. At one point, an assembly of perhaps 200 people was editing the latest Forum communiqué, line by line.

So all this—the plenums, the commissions, the *ad hoc* groups, Havel, John Bok, the *Minotaurus* set, the smoking room, the dressing-rooms, the hasty conversations in the corridors, the heat, the smoke, the laughter and the exhaustion—made up that unique political thing, 'the Magic Lantern'. The story of the revolution, in the days that I witnessed it, was that of the interaction of 'the Magic Lantern' with three other compound forces, or theatres. These may be called, with similar poetic licence, 'the people', 'the powers-that-be' and 'the world'.

For those in the Magic Lantern, 'the people' meant first of all Prague. In a sense, all of Prague became a Magic Lantern. It was not just the great masses on Wenceslas Square. It was the improvised posters all over the city, the strike committees in the factories, the Civic Forum committees that were founded in hospitals, schools and offices. It was the theatres packed every evening for debates with the guest speakers on stage: a Forum spokesman or perhaps an exiled writer, back for the first time in years. It was the crowds standing in front of the television sets in shop or office windows at all hours of the day and night, watching the *Videojournál* tape of the events of 17 November, played over and over again. It was ordinary people on the streets. As you walked down to the old town you overheard snippets of excited conversation: 'Free elections!', 'Human face!' and (darkly) 'Demagogic tendencies!' At six o'clock in the morning on Wenceslas Square you saw a line of hundreds of people waiting patiently in the freezing mist. They were waiting to buy a copy of the Socialist Party newspaper, *Svobodné Slovo* (The Free Word), which was the first to carry accurate reports of the demonstrations and Forum statements. Queueing for the free word.

Outside Prague, the atmosphere was very different from place to place. There was much more fear and nastiness in, for example, the industrial district around Ostrava. And then of course there was Slovakia, a different nation. To reach out to this wider audience the crucial medium was of course television, and to a lesser extent, radio. As in Poland and Hungary, the battle for access to and fair coverage on television and radio was one of the two or three most important political issues. Here, the battle was comically visible on screen, with direct transmission of a demonstration being suddenly interrupted by some inane light music, and then the picture wrenched back—as if by some invisible hand—to the demonstration again. 'Live transmission!' they chanted on Wenceslas Square, 'live transmission!' Once the Forum had access to television and radio, a good deal of its energy was devoted to discussing what to say there.

The second compound force was 'the powers that be'. This term from the King James Bible was repeatedly used by Rita Klimová, a former Professor of Economics (sacked for political reasons) who translated into English for the speakers at the Forum press conferences with magnificent aplomb. At first hearing it may sound quaint, but one of the recurrent problems in describing communist systems (or should I say, former communist systems) is precisely to find an appropriate collective noun for the people and institutions who actually wielded power. To say 'the government', for example, would be wrong, since in such systems the government did not really govern: the Party did, or some mixture of the Party, the police, the army, and the Soviet Union. All these elements were in play, and well described by the biblical term 'the powers that be'.

At the beginning, the Forum negotiated with the federal prime minister, who was also, of course, a politburo member. They did this, in the first place, because he was the only senior power-holder who would talk to them. But, making a virtue of necessity, they said: we are talking to the government of our country because we want a proper government, responsible to a proper parliament, not the rule of one Party. As well as the federal prime minister they also negotiated with the Czech prime minister (for in Czechoslovakia's elaborate federal structure, the Czech lands and Slovakia each have their own governments). Only then did they start talking to Party leaders as such.

Behind everything there was the benign presence of Gorbachev's Soviet Union: the Soviet embassy in Prague receiving a Forum delegation with ostentatious courtesy, Gorbachev himself giving marching orders to Party leader Urbánek and Prime Minister Adamec during the Warsaw Pact post-Malta briefing in Moscow, the renunciation of the 1968 invasion. Others will have to assess how far (and how) Gorbachev deliberately pushed the changes in Czechoslovakia, and to what extent this was affected by his personal timetable of East-West relations, particularly in the run-up to the Malta summit. Just as in 1980 the very worst place from which to assess the Soviet intention to invade was the Solidarity headquarters in Warsaw (a point never entirely grasped by television and radio interviewers) so in 1989 the worst place from which to assess the Soviet intention to do the opposite of invading was the Forum headquarters in Prague. Yet, of course, in a larger historical frame the Soviet attitude was fundamental.

At this point the 'powers that be' shade into the third force, or theatre, called 'the world'. The first protesters in Prague on the national anniversaries in 1988 chanted at the riot police: 'The world sees you.' Yet in the autumn of 1988 it was, in fact, very doubtful if the world did see them. On the whole, the world considered that life was elsewhere. But now there was absolutely no doubt that the world saw them. It saw them through the eyes of the television cameras and the thousands of foreign journalists who flocked into the Magic Lantern for the daily performance. They were a sight in themselves: television crews and photographers behaving like minotaurs, journalists shouting each other down and demanding to know why the revolution could not keep to their deadlines.

Yet a few of the questions were good, and the journalists served two useful functions. First, they concentrated minds. When there was a Forum plenum at, say, five p.m., the knowledge that their spokesmen would have to field the hardest questions at seven-thirty p.m. made for a much sharper discussion: although even then, Forum policy on crucial issues—the future of the Warsaw Pact, for example, or that of socialism—was

93

sometimes made up on the wing, in impromptu answers to Western journalists' questions. Secondly, the 'eyes of the world' offered protection. Particularly in the run-up to the Malta summit, the Czechoslovak authorities must have been left in little doubt that there were certain things that they could no longer do, or could only do at an immense price in both Western and *Soviet* disapproval. Beating children, for example. Both externally and internally, the crucial medium was television. In Europe at the end of the twentieth century all revolutions are telerevolutions.

Day Eight (Friday, 24 November). In the morning, a plenum in the smoking room. Appointing people to the commissions. The agenda for this afternoon's demonstration. The proposed slogans, someone says, are: 'Objectivity, truth, productivity, freedom'. It is no surprise that two out of four have to do with truth. But 'productivity' is interesting. From several conversations outside I can see that the 'Polish example' is widely seen here as a negative one. If economic misery were to be the price for political emancipation, many people might not want to pay it. So the Forum places a premium on economic credibility. Demos only after working hours. The lunch-time general strike on Monday as a one-off necessity.

In the early afternoon comes Dubček. He looks as if he has stepped straight out of a black-and-white photograph from 1968. The face is older, more lined, of course, but he has the same grey coat and paisley scarf, the same tentative, touching smile, the same functionary's hat. Protected by Havel's bodyguards—lead on, John Bok—we emerge from the belly of the Lantern, Dubček and Havel side by side, and scuttle through covered shopping arcades and tortuous back passages to reach the balcony of the Socialist Party publishing house and the offices of *Svobodné Slovo*: the balcony of the free word. Along the arcades people simply gape. They can't believe it. Dubček! It is as if the ghost of Winston Churchill were to be seen striding down the Burlington Arcade.

But when he steps out on to the balcony in the frosty evening air, illuminated by television spotlights, the crowds give such a roar as I have never heard. 'DUBČEK! DUBČEK!' echoes off the tall houses up and down the long, narrow square. Many people mourn his ambiguous role after the Soviet invasion, and his failure to use the magic of his name to support the democratic opposition. He has changed little with the times. His speech still contains those wooden newspeak phrases, the *langue de bois*. (At one point he refers to 'confrontationist extremist tendencies'.) He still believes in socialism—that is, reformed communism—with a human face. The true leader of this movement, in Prague at least, is Havel not Dubček. But for the moment none of this matters. For the moment all that matters is that the legendary hero is really standing here, addressing a huge crowd on Wenceslas Square, while the emergency session of the Central Committee has, we are told, been removed to a distant suburb. 'Dubček to the castle!' roars the crowd—that is, Dubček for president. The old man must believe he will wake up in a moment and find he is dreaming. For the man who supplanted him and now sits in the castle, Gustáv Husák, it is the nightmare come true.

After Dubček comes Havel. 'Dubček-Havel,' they chant, the name of '68 and the name of '89. Then Václav Malý, the banned padre, reads a message from the man he calls 'the third great symbol' of this movement, the ninety-year-old František Cardinal Tomášek. 'The Catholic Church stands entirely on the side of the people in their present struggle,' says the message. 'I thank all those who are fighting for the good of us all and I trust completely the Civic Forum which has become a spokesman for the nation.' 'Long live Tomášek,' they cry, but I notice that when Malý later strikes up the old Czech Wenceslas hymn, much of the crowd either do not know the words or are reluctant to sing them. A striking contrast with Poland.

At the end of the demonstration, after more speakers including a footballer, a theatre director, the rock singer and 'Bridge' member Michael Kocáb, the obligatory Student and Worker, the people down in the square make the most extraordinary spontaneous gesture. They all take their keys out of their pockets and shake them, 300,000 key-rings, producing a sound like massed Chinese bells.

Seven-thirty p.m. The press conference. Havel and Dubček together on stage. They are just starting to field questions about their different ideas of socialism when someone brings the news—from television—that the whole politburo and Central Committee secretariat has resigned. The theatre erupts in applause. Havel leaps to his feet, makes the V-for-Victory sign and embraces Dubček. Someone brings them champagne. Havel raises his glass and toasts 'A free Czechoslovakia!'

Then, rather absurdly, we settle down again to discuss 'What is socialism?' Havel says the word has lost all meaning in 'the Czech lingustic context' over the last fifteen years, but he is certainly in favour of social justice and a plural economy, with different forms of ownership. The models for a rational social policy are to be found rather in social democratic than in communist-ruled countries. The shortest and best answer comes from Václav Malý. I'm also for social justice, he says, but the only way to secure it is through parliamentary democracy.

Ten p.m. Plenum in the smoking room. Operational arrangements for the weekend. There is a need for money: establish a Treasury commission! An interesting discussion about the way in which Dubček should or should not be associated with the Forum. Of course his name is magic, domestically and internationally. But he is, you know, sort of still, well . . . a communist. On every face you see elation fighting a battle against exhaustion. Everyone is very, very tired. At one point, reading a draft declaration about the general strike, the writer Eva Kantůrková says 'Democratic Forum' instead of 'Civic Forum'. 'Oh, sorry, I was thinking of Hungary.' Civic Forum, Democratic Forum, New Forum—Czechoslovakia, Hungary, East Germany— you can easily lose track; it's that kind of year. Someone suggests the general strike should be described as an 'informal referendum' on the leading role of the party. Someone else says 'symbolic', not 'informal'. Writers debate a fine point of style. Agreement by mutual exhaustion. Meeting over.

After midnight. Back in Havel's basement pub, with a wall-painting of a ship in stormy seas. Beer and *becherovka*. What do you talk about on the night after such a tremendous victory, when, in just over a week, you have removed the gibbering thugs who have ruined the country for twenty years? In the first instant, on the stage of Magic Lantern, you may cry 'A free Czecho-slovakia!' But you can't go on talking like characters in a nineteenth-century play. So you suddenly find yourself talking about cats. Yes, cats. Two cats called 'Yin' and 'Yang', whom their owner has not seen for more than a week. Poor things. Victims of the revolution.

So what will happen after the revolution? I ask a beaming Jiří Dientsbier, the star journalist reduced to working as a stoker after signing Charter 77. Quick as ever, he says: 'Either the counter-revolution or ... a Western consumer society.' (Just over two weeks later he is appointed Czechoslovakia's foreign minister. Kindly delete that remark from the record. No, of course you never said that, Mr Minister. Someone else did. I imagined it. It was a voice from the wall.)

Day Nine (Saturday, 25 November). Two Forum statements. One issued after the plenum last night at eleven-thirty p.m. (events move so fast they have not only to date but to time the communiqués) describes the general strike as a 'symbolic referendum' on the leading role. A second, issued at four-thirty a.m., expresses dismay at some of the people elected to the new polit-buro (formally: Presidium) and Central Committee secretariat. The general strike is here described as 'an informal, nationwide referendum on whether or not they should go on humiliating us, and whether this country should continue to be ruined by the leaders of one political party, permanently abrogating to itself the leading role.'

The waiter in my hotel sees me reading *Svobodné Slovo*. 'Ah, victoria!' he says, pointing to the blue, white and red ribbon which he, like so many others, is now wearing in his lapel. Then he leans over and whispers in my ear: 'Finished communism.' Straightening up, he rubs his shoe across the carpet, as if crushing a beetle. Then he takes my *Svobodné Slovo*, but not my breakfast order, and disappears into the kitchen.

This morning there is, by happy chance, a festive mass in the cathedral on the castle hill, to celebrate the canonization of Agnes of Bohemia. The actual canonization took place in Rome on 12 November, just five days before the revolution started. (An old legend has it, so a Catholic friend informs me, that wonders would occur in Bohemia when Agnes was canonized.) In the freezing cold, a large crowd gathers inside and all around the cathedral, and in front of the Archbishop's Palace. 'Frantši Tomášek! Frantši Tomášek!' they chant, a wonderfully chummy way to greet a venerable Cardinal. An old woman quaveringly sings patriotic hymns, pausing only to take a swig of vodka between verses.

The Church here is nothing like the force that it is in Poland, for Czechoslovakia has historically been divided between Catholics (associated with Habsburg counter-reformation and restoration) and Protestants (from Jan Hus to Masaryk), while both churches were ruthlessly suppressed in the Stalinist period, and again after 1969. Yet Catholic intellectuals and banned priests like Václav Malý play a crucial part in the opposition leadership. Tomášek himself has become ever bolder as he gets ever older. The petition for religious freedom last year got more than half a million signatures, and was a major factor in breaking the political ice. And anyway, who could resist the glorious coincidence of this ceremony and the revolution? So there is a goodly crowd here too, some from the countryside and even from Slovakia. And the mass for the patron saint of Bohemia, the king's daughter who came down to live among the poor, is a further celebration of national renewal. Angels at work. Oh yes, and the whole service is broadcast live on television: so far as I can establish, the first time that has ever happened here.

At two p.m., in freezing snow, there is the biggest demonstration of all: over half a million people, in the park near the Letná football stadium, just behind the place where the giant statue of Stalin once stood. With the flags and banners and upturned faces vivid against the white snow, it looks like a painting by L.S. Lowry. Whole sections of the crowd jump up and down together to keep warm. The essential fact is that they are there, at the Forum's invitation. In a sense, that is all that matters. But of course there is a programme.

Havel reiterates the Forum's dissatisfaction with some of the new leaders, and especially with the survival in office of the deeply unpopular Prague Party secretary, Miroslav Štěpán. 'Shame, shame!' cry the crowd. And then he says that the only person in power who had responded to the wishes of the people is the prime minister, Ladislav Adamec. 'Adamec! Adamec!' roar the crowd, and one trembles for a moment at the ease with which they are swayed. This is a quite deliberate (but high-risk) tactic, worked out in the dressing-rooms: to build up the prime minister's position as a negotiating partner by showing to the authorities that he can enjoy popular support. In fact, this is precisely what Adamec asked Havel to do for him a few days ago. Dubček, who, rather to some people's surprise, has not yet returned to Bratislava, repeats the same support for Adamec. He also says, rather nicely, that he is pleased about the canonization of Agnes of Bohemia —Anežka—and that, although he will speak in Slovak, what matters is not how you speak but what you say.

Petr Miller, The Worker, repeats the strike call, stressing once again that it must not damage the national economy. There are ballads and 'President Masaryk's favourite song'; students and actors talk. 'I speak in the name of Jesus Christ,' says one actor, modestly, 'and call upon you to stamp out the devil.' Roars of applause. Then, in the extraordinary way these crowds have of talking back to the speakers, they give an almost instant response 'The devil is in the castle, the devil is in the castle!' (If you stand in the crowd you see how one man can start a chant which, being taken up by those around him, becomes the voice of half a million.)

Seven-thirty p.m. The press conference. Repeating the Forum positions about the compromised leaders, the general strike and so forth. Tomorrow a delegation will meet with Prime Minister Adamec. The agenda is to include the legalization of independent groups, the release of political prisoners, arrangements for further talks, oh yes, and the end of the leading role of the Party. Foreign journalists keep asking them about things they cannot possibly know, such as the power relations inside the Party or the relations between the Soviet and Czechoslovak leadership. Jiří Dienstbier gives a good answer to the last question. Of course we feel the Soviet leadership should have some sense of responsibility for the 1968 invasion, he says, but we are certainly not asking for any more international 'assistance'.

Television is now clearly opening up to report the revolution. Beside the live broadcast of the mass it shows an interview with Havel: down with the leading role, he says, up with free elections. And the crowds outside clearly grasp that as the essential point: 'Free elections,' they chant. As in Poland, in Hungary, in East Germany . . .

Day Ten (Sunday, 26 November). Eleven a.m. A delegation led by Prime Minister Adamec, and formally described as representing the government and National Front (uniting the communist with the formerly puppet parties), meets with a Forum delegation led by Havel. 'We don't know each other,' says the prime minister, extending his hand across the table. 'I'm Havel,' says Havel. It's a short getting-to-know-you session, but they agree to meet again on Tuesday. The prime minister promises the release of political prisoners (many of whom do indeed appear in the Magic Lantern in the course of the day), and also to come to address this afternoon's rally.

Two p.m. At the Letná stadium again. Adamec arrives before the Forum leaders, and stands around stamping his feet in the cold. 'How do you feel?' someone asks him. 'Very nice,' he says, as the crowd roar 'Dubček! Dubček!' I notice his aide trying to suppress a broad grin. Havel delivers a brief speech, describing the Forum as a bridge from totalitarianism to democracy, and saying that it must exist until there are free elections. Then they give Adamec his chance. But he blows it, talking about the need for discipline, for no more strikes, for economic rather than political change. You feel he is talking as much to the emergency Central Committee meeting this evening as to the people in front of him. And they feel it too. They boo and jeer.

The crowd again displays this extraordinary capacity to converse with the speakers in rhythmic chant. 'Make way for the ambulance,' they cry, or 'Turn up the volume.' When a long list of political prisoners is read out they chant, 'Štěpán to prison.' 'Perhaps we should give him a spade,' says Václav Malý from the platform. 'He'd steal it!' comes the almost instantaneous response, half a million speaking as one. And then 'Here it comes!' Sure enough, there is a spade held aloft at the front

102

of the crowd. 'Štěpán, Štěpán,' they cry, as in a funeral chant, and once again they ring their keys, as for the last rites. (Next morning we have the news that Štěpán, along with further discredited members of the leadership, has resigned at the emergency meeting of the Central Committee.)

Six p.m. An important plenum. Havel poses the 'fundamental question' of the future of the Forum. He personally doesn't want to be a 'chief', he says, nor a professional politician. He wants to be a writer. Václav Malý says much the same thing, except that he wants to be—he is—a priest. Yet it is clear to everyone that Havel must carry on at least until the elections, and 'in the elections,' Dienstbier jokes, 'I don't give you any chance!'

Someone else reports telephone calls complaining about undemocratic methods. The old conflict between politics and morality, between the requirements of unity and democracy. The students insist on the need for unity, continuity and Havel's leadership. But other voices are raised in favour of already founding political parties. A social democratic party will announce itself within the next few days. The Forum, everyone agrees, must not be a centralized, party-like organization. What is it then? How do you describe a civic crusade for national renewal?

Inevitably, the discussion swings abruptly between the great and small issues—from what to say to Adamec on Tuesday to what to say to the press in an hour's time, from socialism *vs.* liberalism to whether to go by car or by bus. In the midst of it, Václav Klaus, the glinting economist, suddenly starts to read an amazing document. It is called 'What we want' and subtitled 'Programmatic Principles of the Civic Forum'. It pro-

103

poses a new Czechoslovakia with the rule of law guaranteed by an independent judiciary, free elections at all levels, a market economy, social justice, respect for the environment and independent academic and cultural life. A normal country in the centre of Europe. Three typewritten pages, prepared by one of the commissions in a short weekend. First I saw them sitting on the stage of the Magic Lantern, then sweating away in the dressing-room. My friend Petr Pithart, a lawyer, historian and author of one of the best books about 1968, who was reduced to menial work after signing Charter 77, dropped in to the Magic Lantern to make a modest suggestion. Within minutes he was co-opted on to this commission, writing, in a few hours, a blueprint for a new Czechoslovakia.

When Klaus finishes reading there is a discussion. Václav Benda, a conservative Catholic and one of the original political brains of the Charter, says that although he helped to edit the text he doesn't agree with parts of it: the passage saying that Czechoslovakia will 'respect its international legal obligations' (by implication, including the Warsaw Pact) and another saying that the state should guarantee a social minimum for all. This is a tricky moment, for if the plenum plunges into a serious political discussion then the deep differences that have been covered by the broad yet minimalist platform, first of Charter 77, now of Forum, will surface with a vengeance. Fortunately the moment is saved by Petr Miller, who rises to his feet and says that although he has no higher education he can understand it all, finds it good, and thinks we should just adopt it. In effect: you intellectuals, stop blathering! Sighs of relief all round. A quick vote. Adopted with just three abstentions. Thank heaven for The Worker.

Of course the programme contains passages of fudge: for example, on the Warsaw Pact issue, on the role of the state, and on the ownership question. On the last, it talks of 'real competition' coming about 'on the basis of the parallel existence, with equal rights, of different types of ownership and the progressive opening of our economy to the world'. This is a compromise formula, bearing in mind the sensibilities of the revisionists, social democrats and even Trotskyists who are part of the Forum rainbow coalition, and who still believe in various forms of social(ist) ownership. In effect it says: let the best form win! But privately the economists have absolutely no doubt which form will actually win out.

Yet the truly remarkable thing is not the differences about the programme, but the degree of instant consensus. In 1968, even in 1977, it was almost unthinkable that there would be so much common ground. This is a Czech phenomenon. But it is not just a Czech phenomenon, for in different ways it is repeated all over East Central Europe. Take a more or less representative sample of politically aware persons. Stir under pressure for two days. And what do you get? The same fundamental Western, European model: parliamentary democracy, the rule of law, market economy. And if you made the same experiment in Warsaw or Budapest I wager you would get the same basic result. This is no Third Way. It is not 'socialism with a human face'. It is the idea of 'normality' that seems to be sweeping triumphantly across the world.

But that's enough philosophy. For in the next ten minutes they have to work out what to say to the prime minister—and to the world. At the press conference, they are of course asked about the fudge formulae on the alliances. Dienstbier says: we have to start from the existing situation, but our long-term objective is a Europe without blocs. Spoken like a foreign minister. As for the Soviet Union, this very evening Soviet television is broadcasting a programme about the Prague Spring, including an interview with Dubček. The Dubček interview has been supplied by the samizdat *Videojournál.*

Day Eleven (Monday, 7 November). The general strike is a success almost before it has begun. Television declares it so. Just before noon, the anchorman announces that he is preparing to join in the strike. Then, from the stroke of noon, they show city squares filled with people, in Prague, in Bratislava, in Brno, in Ostrava, wherever, and excited reporters describe the 'fantastic atmosphere'. A sub-title explains that reporting on the strike is the television crews' contribution to the strike. (Yet for the last twenty years they have been grinding out propaganda junk.)

Petr Miller drives me up to his factory, the large ČKD electrotechnical works. Miller drives hair-raisingly fast in his sporty Lada. He enjoys hooting at traffic to let us through, shouting 'Civic Forum!' 'I'm just a very small figure in the opposition,' he says, gesturing with his hand a yard above the ground, to show how small. But in fact he is well on the way to being described as the Czech Wałęsa. On the road we pass an incredible sight: a line of taxis at least one mile long, taxi after taxi after taxi, crawling out up into the hills, wives and girl-friends in the passenger seat. It is the taxi-drivers' strike. In front of the factory gate, the workers are listening patiently to a long lecture on economics by the head of the Prognostic Institute, Dr Valtr Komárek. 'Komárek, Komárek!' they chant. The meeting ends with a singing of the national anthem(s) at one-thirty, so that everyone can be back at work by two. Miller says they will make up the lost work in unpaid overtime. On my way back there is, of course, not a taxi to be found.

Four p.m. A celebration demo on Wenceslas Square. They try to give the platform—or, to be precise, balcony—to a communist. 'Friends, comrades,' he begins, but that is a terrible mistake. 'Boo! Boo!' shout the crowd, and: 'We're not comrades!' Free elections and an end to the leading role of the Party are what people want to hear. Václav Klaus, now emerging as a star of the Forum, reads a statement announcing that the Civic Forum 'considers its basic objective to be the definitive opening of our society for the development of political pluralism and for achieving free elections.' The movement is open to everyone who rejects the present system and accepts the Programmatic Principles. There will be no hierarchical structure, but there will be a 'co-ordinating centre'. The co-ordinating centre recommends the ending of strike action for the time being. Tomorrow they will submit their demand to the prime minister. If he doesn't respond adequately, they will demand the resignation of the government—'Resignation, resignation!' cries the crowd—and the appointment of a new premier willing to assure the holding of a free election. 'Free elections, free elections!'

Then comes the portly, goatee-bearded Dr Komárek who delivers, very slowly and deliberately, what sounds like a prime minister's acceptance speech. There must be deeds not words, he says. 'That's it,' chants the crowd. We need a compromise between the new *de facto* situation and the old *de jure* one. The kids around me giggle at the professorial Latin, but they cry, 'Komárek, Komárek!' There should be a grand coalition government, a government of experts, men of competence

and moral integrity (such as, we understand, Valtr
Komárek). Then a girl student reads out, even more
slowly and clearly, as if in school dictation, a letter from
the students asking the president to replace Adamec
with Komárek. 'Pan Docent Komárek, *Dr.Sc.*,' she says,
has a programme ready. The Forum stands behind him.
'We too,' cry the crowd, 'we too!'

So to everyone standing on that square it is clear that
the Forum—speaking for the people—has just proposed
a candidate for prime minister. Go to the Magic
Lantern, however, and you soon discover that the
Forum didn't mean to do that at all. In the plenum at six
p.m., in the main auditorium now, there is confusion
and consternation. Our position, says Havel, was that
we would give Adamec a chance to meet our demands,
before calling for his resignation. That was the statement Klaus read. The students jumped the gun. Why?
There was a telephone call from the Lantern, say the
students. 'Disinformation!' someone says. 'Provocation!'
Or more likely, just muddle. In any case, the question
now is: what on earth are they to say in the negotiations
with Adamec tommorow? And who should be on the
delegation? A Student, of course. A Worker (Miller).
Ján Čarnogurský, a lawyer and leading Slovak Catholic
activist, just released from prison. Václav Malý.
Perhaps Komárek? 'On whose side?' someone asks. For
Komárek is still a Party member. At this point Havel
slips away off stage. He has to go and collect the Peace
Prize of the German Book Trade. (Four days ago he had
to slip away to collect the Olof Palme Prize.)

Seven-thirty p.m. The press conference. Answers
delivered with great assurance to questions they had
only asked themselves, in this same room, a few
minutes before. No matter. Make it up as you go along.

It's all right on the night. Petr Miller says the strike committees still exist and will be maintained. Not only will they make up the worktime lost by the strike, they'll also work two free Saturdays . . . in the week when Czechoslovakia has free elections. Will there be a Green party? 'This country needs all parties to be green,' says Dienstbier. Well done, Jiří. Spoken like a foreign minister again. But now he has to dash: his boilers need stoking.

Day Twelve (Tuesday, 28 November). At half past one a government minister, one Marián Čalfa, gives the first account of the negotiations between the government/National Front team under Adamec, and the Forum delegation under Havel. The meeting started in an 'excited' atmosphere, he says. But then it settled down and ended in a 'positive' spirit. The prime minister promised, by Sunday (3 December), to put together a new government based on 'a broad coalition', a government of experts. The government will propose to the Federal Assembly that the clauses about the leading role of the Party, the subordinate nature of the National Front, and Marxism-Leninism as the basis of education, should be removed from the constitution. The prime minister also promised that the City Council would provide the Forum with all facilities.

According to people on the Forum side, Adamec actually lost his cool on being confronted with the Forum's demands—a short digest of those raised by the students and the people over the last week. He called them 'an ultimatum'. After a short break, Petr Miller once again defused the situation with some straight talking.

Four p.m. Plenum. Perhaps 200 people in the auditorium. Havel and other delegation members on stage.

109

The main subject: the Forum's version of the meeting. As well as the three points accepted by the government that all political prisoners should be released by 10 December (UN Human Rights Day), there was an expression of satisfaction at the establishment of a parliamentary commission to investigate the police and security forces' violence on 17 November. The draft read out by Radim Palouš includes five more points. Of these the most immediately dramatic is the announcement that they are writing to President Husák, calling upon him to resign by 10 December. The prime minister has until the end of the year to make clear the way in which his new government will create the legal conditions for free elections, freedom of assembly, association, speech and press, the end of state control over the churches etc. In addition, the People's Militia, the Party's private army, must be dissolved and all political organizations removed from the workplace (as in Hungary). If not, they will demand his resignation.

After the draft is read, Havel says, 'Now I leave you to discuss it,' and scuttles off backstage, through the Minotaur's hole. In the course of a rather confused discussion, Petr Pithart sharply points out that they have not actually said anything about the composition of the new government. What about the crucial levers of power, the interior and defence ministries, for example? From the platform comes the slightly sheepish reply: yes, but we can't really say something here that we didn't mention there. Somehow, in the rush and muddle, that point didn't get made. Ah well. Once again, Petr Miller ends the intellectual discussion: let's accept it now, he says, we can always elaborate later.

Press conference. The final version of the communiqué—as edited by the 200!—is read out. So is the text of a letter to the Soviet authorities about the reassessment of 1968. This, they report, was accepted 'with pleasure' by the Soviet Embassy, who promised that it would promptly be sent to Moscow by telex. Asked about the negotiations, Havel says they were complicated, fast, dramatic, and please don't expect all the details here. Altogether, he pleads to be left alone by the press. All questions to him, he says, he will gladly answer at an all-day press conference—after the revolution.

Day Thirteen (Wednesday, 29 November). Television broadcasts a speech by the new Party secretary, Karel Urbánek, attempting to cheer up the Party faithful at an emergency *aktiv* in the Palace of Culture. He adopts a fighting tone. We will not sell out to foreign capital like the Poles! We cannot concede to demands to dissolve the People's Militia! (On Saturday, they will do just that.) The audience chants 'Urbánek, Urbánek!' and 'Long live the KSČ!' in the rhythms of the crowd on Wenceslas Square.

Then the Federal Assembly. The women with putty faces, cheap perms and schoolmistress voices. The men in cheap suits, with hair swept straight back from sweaty foreheads. The physiognomy of power for the last forty years. But at the end of the day they all vote 'yes' to the prime minister's proposal, as agreed yesterday with the Forum, to delete the leading role of the Party from the constitution, and remove Marxism-Leninism as the basis of education. For years, for a lifetime in some cases, they have been preaching Marxism-Leninism and the leading role. But no single deputy votes against the change. As Orwell said: Once a whore, always a whore.

Four p.m. Plenum, in the auditorium. Havel and a

delegation have hurried off to Bratislava, to speak in the Slovak National Theatre. It is vital not to let the authorities divide Slovaks against Czechs, as they have done so often in the past. Yesterday's communiqué about the meeting with the government underlined the fact that this was a negotiation by the Civic Forum and the Public Against Violence, the sister organization in Slovakia. And the first item of today's communiqué records their common resolution: 'The common objective of the CF and the PAV is the changing of Czecho-slovakia into a democratic federation, in which Czechs and Slovaks, together with other nationalities, will live in mutual friendship and understanding.' Yet there are rocks ahead on this road. For the issue is not just democracy as such; it is also the degree of self-government to be enjoyed by the two nation(alitie)s within the federal state.

But before anyone can discuss this a group of students come on stage, dressed comically as young pioneers: white blouses, red bows, the girls' hair in pigtails. It is the Committee For A More Joyful Present. We have come, they say, to cheer you up—and to make sure that you don't turn into another politburo. Then they hand out little circular mirrors to each member of the plenum.

Back to business. Point three reads: 'The prime min-ister in yesterday's negotiations with the CF said that he wished to discuss with us the members of the new cabinet. The CF does not aspire to any ministerial post, but would like to suggest to the prime minister that the minister of national defence be a civilian who has not compromised himself and is a member of the Com-munist Party of Czechoslovakia, while the minister of the interior be a person who has not compromised

112

himself, is a civilian and is not a member of the Party. This suggestion was given to the prime minister in the course of this morning.' In fact the suggestion came, drafted by Havel, from his dressing-room to the 'crisis staff' dressing-room, and was agreed within a few minutes. A little afterthought: oh, and by the way, you can't have the interior ministry any more!

Who wants to speak at the press conference? No takers. People have to be press-ganged to face the press.

Should we talk about this as a revolution? someone asks. For after all, in our linguistic context the word 'revolution' has a clear sub-text of violence. A 'peaceful revolution' sounds like a contradiction in terms. A rather academic point, you might think. But actually a great deal of what is happening is precisely about words: about finding new, plain, true words rather than the old mendacious phrases with which people have lived for so long. The drafting committees try to ensure that from the outset the Forum's statements are in fresh language. Alas, they do not always succeed. The communiqués, with their repetition of acronyms ('CF and PAV'), soon begin to sound like old officialese.

Seven-thirty p.m. Press conference. Václav Klaus smilingly reports a press interview with the deposed Party leader, Miloš Jakeš, in which he said that the Forum is well organized. 'I'm sorry to say,' Klaus comments, 'that even on this point we can't agree with him.' The issue of academics sacked after 1969. We are already drawing up a list of those who should be reinstated, says a student leader. But how would they find places for them? 'I can assure you that we have quite enough very incompetent professors . . . '

Day Fourteen (Thursday, 30 November). Four p.m.

Plenum. The internal organization of the Forum 'co-ordinating centre'. Ivan Havel, whose subject is cybernetics, has produced a most impressive and logical plan, now displayed on a blackboard on stage. Suddenly the theatre looks like a lecture room: the revolution has become a seminar.

One of the issues being discussed in the seminar is how to change the composition of the Federal Assembly, or parliament. Once again, there is the conflict between the moral imperative of democracy and the political imperative of swift, effective action. There is a legal provision by which members of parliament can be 'recalled', that is, removed, on a vote of the parliament itself, and replaced by new, nominated—not freely elected—members. This method was used to purge the parliament after the Soviet invasion. Now Professor Jičinský, a constitutional lawyer who was himself removed from the parliament by this method, proposes to hoist the communists with their own petard. Others say: But this is undemocratic, there should at least be free elections in the vacated constituencies (as, incidentally, has happened in Hungary). But this would take much longer, and time is what they do not have. A more representative assembly is needed now. So can you take an undemocratic short-cut to democracy?

Meanwhile, a Forum delegation has the first direct, bilateral meeting with Party leaders. The Party side is led by Vasil Mohorita, who, as head of the official youth movement, licensed the students' demonstration that started it all, and then agreed a statement condemning the use of violence against the demonstrators. Perhaps he is the looked-for partner in the Party?

After the television news, there is a long interview with Zdeněk Mlynář, a leading member of the Dubček leadership in 1968. He was invited to Prague from his exile in Vienna by the new Party leader, Karel Urbánek, and rushed in to a meeting with him after crossing the border in the dead of night. In their desperation, the Party leaders are turning for advice to, and hoping to win back, the old communists whom they expelled (some half a million of them) and defamed after the invasion. Mlynář is introduced on television as a 'political scientist from Innsbruck'. He gives a highly eloquent performance, stressing the importance of Gorbachev and the whole international context, as at all the previous turning-points in Czechoslovakia's history, in 1918, in 1938, in 1948, in 1968. What he does not spell out are the concrete steps needed to dismantle the communist system. At the end of the interview you feel that he is still ultimately pleading, like Dubček, for the concepts of 1968, for a reformed communism called 'socialism with a human face'—in short, for an idea whose time has gone.

Later in the evening, I walk with the theatre director Petr Oslzlý through the impossibly beautiful streets of the old town, to the small Theatre on a Balustrade, where Havel's first plays were performed in the early sixties. Today, like all the other theatres, it hosts an improvised happening. After a short talk by an economist, and a discussion with an exiled choreographer about how theatres are financed in the West, there is a Czech Country and Western group. In what might be called Czenglish they sing: 'I got ol' time religion . . . '

Day Fifteen (Friday, 1 December). Pavel Bratinka sits in his stoker's hut at the metro building site, with a huge pile of coal outside the door, a makeshift bed, junk-shop furniture, and he says: 'On the whole I favour a bicameral legislature.' He has been studying these

115

issues for years, politics and law and economics, writing articles for the underground press, and occasionally for Western publications. With him, one has that rare experience of someone who has really thought everything through for themselves, not taking anything for granted. He is therefore unmatchably confident of the positions he takes up: positions which in American terms would be considered neo-conservative. I have known him for several years, and treasured his explosive intellectual wrath. But this conversation is different. For while we still sit in the grimy hut, Pavel in his enormous, leather-reinforced stoker's trousers, I think that, within a few months, he will be sitting, in a smart suit, in the new lower house of a real parliament.

Five p.m. Plenum. Several people have been nominated already for the 'crisis staffs' over the weekend. Are there any more volunteers? This is a critical weekend, since Sunday is the deadline set by the Forum for the announcement of the new government, and they will then have to react to Adamec's list. Effectively, almost anyone who wants to from among this miscellaneous group could appoint themselves to participate in the crucial decision. But everyone is simply exhausted after a fortnight of revolution. Their wives and children are complaining. And damn it, it is the weekend. So the list of volunteers grows only slowly.

The meeting wakes up when a burly farmer arrives, having just successfully disrupted an official congress of agricultural co-operatives. He reads out—no, he elocutes—a rousing statement, beginning, 'We the citizens...' and covering everything from freedom to fertilizers. Then he asks for speakers from the Forum to come out into the countryside. People in the country, he says, think Charter 77 is a group of former prisoners.

After seven, Havel and Petr Pithart return, also exhausted, from five hours of negotiations with the Czech (as opposed to the federal) prime minister. Here too, the central issue was the composition of a new government, and changes in those arrangements (e.g. for education) which are within the competence of this body. Finally they have agreed a joint communiqué, after arguing for an hour over one word—the word 'resignation'. You must understand what it means for these people, says Havel, to sign a joint communiqué with us, who for twenty years they have regarded—or at least treated—as dangerous criminals.

The early hours. The king of Bohemia arrives back in his basement pub. 'Ah, *pane* Havel!' cries a girl at a neighbouring table, and sends over her boy-friend to get an autograph on a cigarette packet. Havel is a Bohemian in both senses of the word. He is a Czech intellectual from Bohemia, with a deep feeling for his native land. But he is also an artist, nowhere happier than in a tavern with a glass of beer and the company of pretty and amusing friends. Short, with light hair and moustache, and a thick body perched on small feet, he looks younger than his fifty-three years. Even in quieter times, he is a bundle of nervous energy, with hands waving like twin propellers, and a quite distinctive, almost Chaplinesque walk: short steps, slightly stooping, a kind of racing shuffle. He wears jeans, open shirts, perhaps a corduroy jacket, only putting on a suit and tie under extreme duress: for example, when receiving one of those international prizes. Negotiations with the government, by contrast, do not qualify for a suit and tie. His lined yet boyish face is constantly breaking into a winning smile, while from inside this small frame a surprisingly deep voice rumbles out some wry remark.

117

Despite appearances, he has enormous stamina. Few men could have done half of what he has done in the last fortnight and come out walking, let alone talking. Yet here he is, at one o'clock in the morning, in his local, laughing as if he made revolutions every week.

Day Sixteen (Saturday, 2 December). A shabby back room, with a broken-down bed and a girlie calendar on the wall. On one side, the editors of a samizdat—but soon to be legal—paper. On the other side, Havel, František Janouch, the head of the Stockholm-based Charter 77 Foundation, and, from Vienna, Prince Karl von Schwarzenberg, the chairman of the International Helsinki Federation, with tweed jacket and Sherlock Holmes pipe. Arrangements are to be made for the newly legal paper. The Prince takes note of their needs. At one point, there is talk of some fiscal permission required. Havel takes a typewritten list of names out of his bag, and finds the name of the finance minister. 'Does anyone know him?' he jokes. Silence. Schwarzenberg says: 'What kind of country is this, where one doesn't know the minister?'

Suddenly people have badges saying 'Havel for President'. They are made, I am told, in Hungary. Havel says shyly, 'May I have one?' and pops it in his pocket.

In the evening there is a ceremony on the stage of the Magic Lantern to thank the staff for their help, since on Monday they are to resume more normal performances. After short speeches, the lights go down, a fireworks display is projected on to the backdrop, and everyone joins in singing the Czech version of 'We Shall Overcome', swaying from side to side with hands raised in the V-for-Victory sign. Then we drink pink champagne. Emerging from the auditorium, I see a solitary figure standing in the foyer, with half-raised glass, indecisively, as if pulled in four directions at once by invisible arms. It is Havel. We sit down on a bench and he rumbles confidentially: 'I am just engaged in very important negotiations about...'—at which point a pretty girl comes up with another bottle of champagne. Then someone with an urgent message. Then another pretty girl. Then Prince Schwarzenberg. I never do get his account of those vital negotiations.

Day Seventeen (Sunday, 3 December). Another stage, another inaugural meeting, this time of the new writers' union, in the Realistic Theatre. Havel says a few words, and is just slipping away when they haul him back on stage and tell him he must be chairman of the new union. Elected by acclamation, he makes his racing shuffle to the microphone and says thank you, yes, thank you, and he is frightfully sorry but he really has to dash... which he certainly does, for they are about to make known the proposed composition of Adamec's new government.

And a very bad composition it is too. After Adamec's solemn declaration about proposing a 'broad coalition' government of experts, and after the deletion of the leading role of the Party from the constitution, no less than sixteen out of the twenty-one proposed members of the government are Party members. Amongst them are almost no experts, but instead some very compromised figures, such as the foreign minister, Jaromír Johanes. Clearly this is unacceptable.

Crisis meeting in the smoking room. What is to be done? Some say that the Forum must go for what the people obviously want: a real government of experts led by Komárek. Others say that is impossible, and Komárek not the right man. Professor Jičinský, the constitutional lawyer, points out that the Forum is in

119

danger of painting itself into a constitutional corner: for if they don't accept the government, and demand the president's resignation by next Sunday, then they could end up with no constitutional authority in the land except the old and corrupt parliament. A confused discussion ends in general agreement that the Forum must demand the further reconstruction of the government, backing this up with a demonstration on Wenceslas Square tomorrow afternoon, and the threat of a general strike on Monday week. Petr Pithart, now a central figure, is chosen to deliver the Forum's reaction on television this evening, along with a student, an actor, and Petr Miller to add the worker's muscle. They hurry off down into the stuffy, boiling dressing-rooms to draft the statements, with the master-draftsman, Havel. Now there is no pink champagne and no laughter. It is too serious a business.

But later in the evening there is a moment, if not for laughter, then at least for a quiet tear. There is a concert 'for all right-thinking people', a concert to celebrate the revolution. When Marta Kubišová comes on stage, the audience erupts in the kind of applause that usually only follows a brilliant performance. But they are not applauding her singing. They are applauding her silence. Nearly twenty years of silence. For Marta Kubišová, one of the most popular singers of the sixties, and a folk-heroine of '68, has not been allowed to appear in public in her native land since 1970. When the applause finally subsides, a girl presents her with a bunch of flowers, 'one for each lost year'. A fragile, gentle figure, now in early middle age, Marta Kubišová is so overwhelmed that she can hardly speak, let alone sing. 'Thank you, thank you,' she whispers into the microphone. Then, with a friend supporting her, she sings: 'The times they are a changin'...' It is a moment of joy, but with a core of bitter sadness. For to most of her audience the songs she sings are ancient history—the sounds of the sixties.

Day Eighteen (Monday, 4 December). Three-forty-five p.m. Wenceslas Square. Despite the freezing cold, the demonstration will be huge, and a success. Of course it will. Everyone knows it. They file into the square slowly and matter-of-factly, as if they had been doing it for years. A few minutes before four, they start warming up with the familiar chants: 'Now's the time!', 'Resignation!', and ringing the keys. 'Long live the students!' they cry—is there another city in the world where you would hear that?—and 'Long live the actors!' Then come the official—that is, official unofficial—speakers, slowly reading rather complicated statements, full of 'CF and PAV'. 'Long live the Forum!' they chant, regardless. Loud support for the general strike on 11 December. A fine, theatrical performance by Radim Palouš, who reads out the proposal to recall compromised members of the Federal Assembly, namely, he says—pause—and then, like a whiplash, 'Jakeš.' Whistles and jeers. And so on down the list of gibbering thugs: Fojtík, Indra, Bilak. 'Let it be done,' says the crowd. And from one corner: 'Do it like the Germans!' (Meaning the East Germans, for this morning brought the news of Erich Honecker *et al* being expelled from the Party and placed under house arrest.) But 'like the Germans' is how the Forum leaders do not want to do it. They want to do it like the Czechs, that is, gently, tolerantly, without hatred and revenge.

Finally, the bell-clear voice of Václav Malý, reading the Forum statement: the demand for free elections by the end of June 1990 at the latest, with the new indication that the Forum will propose or endorse candidates; the formation of a genuine coalition government by next Sunday, otherwise the Forum will propose its own candidate; the Forum and the PAV in Slovakia declaring themselves to be the guarantors of the transition to a democratic state based on the rule of law. 'Long live the Forum!' Then, in a last touch which verges on kitsch, the pudgy pop star Karel Gott (a housewives' darling) and the exiled Karel Kryl come out on to the balcony together, to lead the singing of the national anthem(s), the slow, heart-rending first verse in Czech, the sprightly, dance-rhythm second verse in Slovak.

I walk back up the road to my hotel, where the television brings news of the successful Malta summit, of Gorbachev's subsequent meeting with Warsaw Pact leaders in Moscow, and then, separately, with Urbánek and Adamec. There is a report about the round-up of communist leaders in East Germany. Later, a flash: the five Warsaw Pact states which invaded Czechoslovakia in 1968 have formally renounced and condemned this as an intervention in Czechoslovakia's internal affairs.

So every schoolboy can see which way the external winds are blowing. No doubt this will be a week of tense and tortuous negotiation. But it is hard to see what alternative the authorities have, other than to make further concessions. They are caught between the hammer of popular revolt and the anvil of a completely transformed external context, symbolized by the Malta summit and that Warsaw Pact statement. 'From Yalta to Malta' for the world, from Husák to Havel for Prague.

A late-night walk through the old town, veiled in mist. After twenty long years, the sleeping beauty of Central Europe has woken up. The improvised posters

122

on the shop windows deserve an article in themselves.
'Unity is strength,' they say. 'People, open your eyes.'
And: 'The heart of Europe cries for freedom.'

At this point the Forum had to leave the Magic Lantern
and I had, alas, to leave Prague. The next week was
probably as important as the previous two, but someone
else will have to chronicle its inner dramas. On the
Tuesday there were further, inconclusive talks with
Adamec. On Wednesday he threatened to resign, and on
Thursday he did so. His former deputy, Marián Čalfa, a
Slovak, was asked by President Husák to form a new
government. The Forum said they might be able to come
to an agreement with him, and made some 'suggestions'
for the new cabinet. (A week before they had said 'the CF
does not aspire to any ministerial post', but a week in
revolutionary politics is a very long time.)

There followed 'round table' talks between representatives of all the official parties—crucially, of
course, the communists, headed here by Vasil Mohorita
—and those of the Forum, headed by Havel, and of the
Public Against Violence, headed by Ján Čarnogurský.
As in Poland, the 'round table' really had two sides. In
Poland, the round table lasted two months; in Czechoslovakia, two days. Precisely to the Forum's deadline,
on Sunday, 10 December, UN Human Rights Day,
Gustáv Husák swore in the new government and then
resigned as president.

Václav Havel read out the names of the new cabinet to
a jubilant crowd on Wenceslas Square. Virtually all the
Forum's 'suggestions' were reflected in the agreed list.
Ján Čarnogurský was catapulted in the space of just a
fortnight from being a prisoner of conscience, expecting a
stiff sentence, to being one of two so-called 'first vice-

premiers' of Czechoslovakia, with partial responsibility for the security apparatus that had so long harassed and persecuted him. In a compromise, since the two sides could not agree on an interior minister, he would initially share this responsibility with the premier, Marián Čalfa, and the other 'first vice-premier', our old friend the chief Prognostic, Pan Docent Valtr Komárek, *Dr.Sc.* Komárek would have overall responsibility for economic policy, with under him two other members of his institute: Vladimír Dlouhý (like Komárek, a Party member), and, predictably, Václav Klaus, the glinting Friedmanite, as Minister of Finance. (So now Prince Schwarzenberg could rest content: one *does* know the minister.)

As if in a fairy tale, Jiří Dienstbier went from stoker to Foreign Minister. Almost as remarkably, Miroslav Kusý, a well-known Slovak philosopher and Charter 77 signatory, expelled from the Party like so many others, took charge of the Federal Office of Press and Information. Petr Miller, the Worker, became Minister for Labour and Social Affairs. The formerly puppet, but newly independent, Socialist and People's parties got two seats each. Although the prime minister was still a communist, only eight other ministers (out of a total twenty-one) were Party members, and of these, two— Komárek and Dlouhý—were identified more with the Forum than with the Party.

It was an extraordinary triumph at incredible speed. The next day's general strike was of course cancelled: instead the factory sirens blew and church bells rang. Within the next week, Klaus and Čarnogurský were already announcing fiscal and legal changes to start the country down the road to a market economy and the rule of law: the road conjured up seemingly out of nothingness in those steamy dressing-rooms and corri-

dors of the Magic Lantern just a fortnight before. Next
Sunday, Jiří Dienstbier was cutting the barbed wire of
the iron curtain on the Czechoslovak-Austrian frontier,
holding the giant wire-cutters with his colleague, the
Austrian foreign minister, Alöis Mock. The students
held another demonstration, taking exactly the same
route that they had done on Day One, just a month
before: along the embankment, right at the National
Theatre, up Narodní avenue into Wenceslas Square.
This time they were not met by truncheon-wielding
police, by white helmets or red berets, for this time the
police were, in a real sense, under their control.

As in Poland and Hungary, one outstanding issue was
the election of a new president. The Forum soon decided
that Havel was its candidate, for the transitional period
to free elections, and that he should be elected as soon as
possible by the Federal Assembly. The Party, by contrast, suddenly discovered a burning passion for democracy, and said the next president should be elected by
direct popular vote, which would take longer to organize, and which, it fondly hoped, Havel might actually
lose. (Note that the Hungarian party had tried to play
exactly the same game.) There was also an important
side-play concerning a suitable position for Dubček,
with his importance as an historical symbol, a reform
communist and, not least, a Slovak. But both disputes
were swiftly resolved by negotiations between the
Forum and the Party, and between Havel and Dubček
in person. They agreed that Dubček should become the
Chairman of the Federal Assembly, and Havel should
be president. The Party had to swallow both, the man of
'68 and the man of '89.

On 28 December the Federal Assembly elected
Dubček, and on 29 December, with Dubček in the chair,

at a festive ceremony in the coronation hall of Prague Castle, Václav Havel was elected president of what was still called the Czechoslovak Socialist Republic. There followed a high mass in the Cathedral, conducted by the man whom Václav Malý had described as the third great symbol of these events, Cardinal František Tomášek. In the evening there was a splendid party, and people danced in the streets. They had a second president-liberator in Masaryk's chair.

Of course there were countless difficulties ahead on the path to the free elections scheduled for June 1990. Yet barring a great disaster (external or internal) it none the less seemed certain that Czechoslovakia was now launched down the same road as Poland and Hungary, as East Germany (in a special, complicated way) and perhaps Bulgaria and Romania: the road from communism to democracy. The breakthrough had happened.

The 'ten days' took twenty-four. What I have recounted here is only a small part of the story, albeit a central part. There are many other vital parts that others will have to fill in: for example, the story from the Party-government side and, indeed, the detail of the actual negotiations. It is too soon to draw up a balance-sheet. But a few tentative reflections may already be ventured.

Why did it happen in November? The real question is rather: why did it not happen before? Historically, Czechoslovakia was much the most democratic state in the region before the war. Geographically, Prague lies west of Vienna. Culturally, it is *the* Central European city. The gulf between the *pays réel* and the surreal, mendacious *pays légal*—Husák's kingdom of forgetting —grew ever wider. In the last couple of years, the number of those prepared to risk something in order to speak their real minds grew very significantly. There were the hundreds of thousands of believers who signed the petition for religous freedom. There were the 40,000 who signed the 'Several Sentences' manifesto. There were the students and the actors. Once the transformations began in neighbouring Poland and Hungary, one had the feeling that it was just a matter of time before things moved in Czechoslovakia.

And so it was. But East Germany went first. And if one asks, 'Why did the revolution go so fast in Czechoslovakia?' then the simple answer is 'because the Czechs came last.' East Germany was the final straw: seen, remember, not just on television but also in Prague itself, as the East German escapees flooded into the West German embassy. National pride was aroused. Rapid change was clearly possible and allowed, even encouraged, by Gorbachev. Everyone was ready. From the audience in the Realistic Theatre on the first Saturday who immediately leapt to their feet in a standing ovation at the actors' demand for a general strike, to the crowds on Wenceslas Square chanting 'Now's the time', from the journalists who at once started reporting truthfully to the workers who never hesitated about going on strike: everyone was ready. Everyone knew, from their neighbours' experience, that it could be done.

More than that, their neighbours had given them a few ideas about how it should be done. In a real sense, Czechoslovakia was the beneficiary, and what happened there the culmination, of a ten-year-long Central European learning process—with Poland being the first, but paying the heaviest price. A student occupation strike? Of course, as in Poland! Non-violence? The first commandment of all Central European oppositions. Puppet parties coming alive? As in East Germany. A 'round table' to negotiate the transition? As in Poland and Hungary. And so on. Politically, Czechoslovakia had what economic historians call the 'advantages of backwardness'. They could learn from the others' examples; and from their mistakes.

Yet when all this has been said, no one in Prague could resist the feeling that there must also be an additional, supra-rational cause at work. Hegel's *Weltgeist*, said some. Agnes of Bohemia, said others. 'The whole world is moving from dictatorship to democracy,' said a third, in a newspaper interview. How you describe the supra-rational agency is a matter of personal choice. For myself, I'll stick with the angels.

If there were angels at work, there were also devils. One saw more than once how the devils of ambition, vanity, pride, the little germs of corruption, wriggled their way down into the bowels of the Magic Lantern. Taken all in all, however, the central assembly of the Forum in the Czech lands was an impressive body. It was as democratic as it could reasonably be, in the circumstances. It was remarkably good-humoured. It showed a genius for improvisation. Profound differences of political orientation, faith and attitudes were generally subordinated to the common good. A reasonable balance was struck between the political and the moral imperatives. Above all, men and women who for twenty years had been deprived of the most basic possibilities of political articulation were able to get together and say, within a matter of days: 'This is what we want, this is how the face of the new Czechoslovakia should look.' And it is a face that bears examination.

All the same, they were very lucky. Even by comparison with the opposition movements in Poland,

Hungary and East Germany, this was the politics of amateurs. There were several moments in the second week when one felt they had lost their way in the tangle of demands, long- and short-term, moral, symbolic and political. To forget about those crucial levers of power, the defence and interior ministries, in a discussion of the composition of the new government might look, to a cold and critical observer, like carelessness. To toss in the demand next day, in a hastily drafted letter, might look, to the cold and critical observer, like theatre rather than politics. But such was the tide of popular feeling, and so favourable the external winds, that it came right in the end.

'Unhappy the land that has need of heroes,' cries Brecht's Galileo. Unhappy the land that has need of revolutions. The twenty years, and in many respects the forty years, were really lost. Lives had been ruined. Damage had been done that could never be repaired. But if a land has to have a revolution, then it would be difficult to imagine a better revolution than the one Czechoslovakia had: swift, almost entirely non-violent, joyful and funny. A laughing revolution. It came without the accompanying (and precipitating) economic crisis of Poland or Hungary. What is more, because the change was so swift—because within a month, Komárek, Dlouhý and Klaus were already in government, taking the necessary steps—Czechoslovakia had a real chance of making the larger transition from dictatorship to democracy, and from planned to market economy, with relatively less economic pain than its neighbours: although I stress the word 'relatively'.

So at Christmas time my parting images had to be of happiness. Collective happiness, as seen on Wenceslas Square, but even more of individual happiness. I

129

thought of Pavel, designing the bicameral legislature in his stoker's hut. I thought of Petr, given a new last chapter for his history of Czechoslovakia, which would be published legally. I thought of Rita, preparing for her new job as ambassador to Washington. I thought of Jiří, now making the foreign policy of the Czechoslovak (Socialist?) Republic. And I thought of Václav—that is, Wenceslas—drinking a Christmas toast.

Sentimental? Absurdly so. But sufficient unto the day are the evils thereof. For a few days at least we could surely rejoice. The ice had thawed. After twenty years, the clocks had started again in Prague. The most Western of all the so-called East European countries was resuming its proper history.

The Year of Truth

This was the year communism in Eastern Europe died. 1949-1989 R.I.P. And the epitaph might be:

Nothing in his life
Became him like the leaving it

The thing that was comprehensively installed in the newly defined territories of Poland, Czechoslovakia, Hungary, Romania and Bulgaria, and in the newly created German Democratic Republic after 1949, the thing called, according to viewpoint, 'socialism', 'totalitarianism', 'Stalinism', 'politbureaucratic dictatorship', 'real existing socialism', 'state capitalism', 'dictatorship over needs', or, most neutrally, 'the Soviet-type system' —that thing will never walk again. And arguably, if we can no longer talk of communism we should no longer talk of Eastern Europe, at least with a capital 'E' for Eastern. Instead, we shall have central Europe again, east central Europe, south-eastern Europe, eastern Europe with a small 'e' and, above all, individual peoples, nations and states.

To be sure, even without a political-military reversal inside the Soviet Union there will be many further conflicts, injustices and miseries in these lands. But they will be different conflicts, injustices and miseries: new and old, post-communist but also pre-communist. In the worst case, there might yet be new dictators; but they would be different dictators. We shall not see again that particular system, characterized by the concentration of political and economic power and the instruments of coercion in the hands of one Leninist party, manifested sociologically as a privileged new class, in states with arbitrarily limited sovereignty.

Of course if we walk the streets of Prague, Warsaw or Leipzig we can still find the grey, familiar traces: the flattened neo-classical Stalinist façades on all the Victory Squares, the Lenin boulevards, steelworks, shipyards, the balding middle-aged officials with their prefabricated lies, the cheap paper forms for completion in quadruplicate, the queues, the attitude of 'We pretend to work and you pretend to pay us'. Yet even the physical evidences are being removed at a speed that must cause some anxiety to conservationists. (In Poland there is a scheme for preserving all the old props in an entertainment park. The proposed name is Stalinland.)

If 1989 was the end, what was the beginning of the end? To read the press, or hear Mrs Thatcher talk, you would think history began with Gorbachev. At the other extreme, some would say communism in Eastern Europe was doomed at birth. This thesis may, in turn, be advanced in several forms. One can say that communism was incompatible with the political culture of East Central Europe, although why that political culture should suddenly stop at the quite arbitrary western frontier of the Soviet Union is not clear. Alternatively, one can say that communism was a wonderful idea that was doomed only because the people of Eastern Europe did not find their way to it themselves, but had it imposed on them by a foreign power, which itself did not understand it. Or one can say that communism is incompatible with human nature, period. Whether by congenital deformity or merely as the result of a ghastly forceps delivery, the death was preordained at birth. In between these two extreme positions, some people in the countries concerned would point to various supposed 'missed opportunities' or turning-points at which East European history failed to turn. 1956 and 1968 are the leading candidates in this class.

As usual, there is an element of truth in all these claims, though in some more than others. Churchill declared, 'I have not become the King's First Minister in order to preside over the liquidation of the British empire,' and proceeded to do almost exactly that. Gorbachev came to power proposing to save the Soviet empire and presides over its disintegration. That Moscow permitted the former 'satellite' countries to determine how they want to govern themselves was clearly a *sine qua non*. But the nature and direction of the processes of domestic political self-determination cannot be understood by studying Soviet policy. The causes lie elsewhere, in the history of individual countries, in their interactions with their East European neighbours and with the more free and prosperous Europe that lies to the west, north and south of them.

If I was forced to name a single date for the 'beginning of the end' in this *inner* history of Eastern Europe, it would be June 1979. The judgement may be thought excessively Polonocentric, but I do believe that the Pope's first great pilgrimage to Poland was that turning-point. Here, for the first time, we saw that massive, sustained, yet supremely peaceful and self-disciplined manifestation of social unity, the gentle crowd against the Party-state, which was both the hallmark and the essential domestic catalyst of change in 1989, in every country except Romania (and even in Romania, the violence did not initially go out from the crowds). The Pope's visit was followed, just over a year later, by the birth of Solidarity, and without the Pope's visit it is doubtful if there would have been a Solidarity.

The example of Solidarity was seminal. It pioneered a new kind of politics in Eastern Europe (and new not only there): a politics of social self-organization and negotiating the transition from communism. The players, forms and issues of 1980-81 in Poland were fundamentally different from anything seen in Eastern Europe between 1949 and 1979: in many respects, they presaged those seen throughout Eastern Europe in 1989. If there is any truth in this judgement, then there was something especially fitting in the fact that it was in 1989 that the Russian leader and the Polish Pope finally met. In their very different ways, they both started it.

To find a year in European history comparable with 1989, however, we obviously have to reach back much farther than 1979, or 1949. 1789 in France? 1917 in Russia? Or, closer to home, 1918/19 in Central Europe? But 1918/19 was the aftermath of World War. The closer parallel is surely 1848, the springtime of nations. In the space of a few paragraphs such comparisons are little better than parlour games. Yet, like parlour games, they can be amusing, and may sometimes help to concentrate the mind.

1848 erupted, according to A.J.P. Taylor, 'after forty years of peace and stability' while Lewis Namier describes it, with somewhat less cavalier arithmetic, as 'the outcome of thirty-three creative years of European peace carefully preserved on a consciously counter-revolutionary basis.' The revolution, Namier writes, 'was born at least as much of hopes as of discontents.' There was undoubtedly an economic and social background: lean harvests and the potato disease. But 'the common denominator was ideological.' He quotes the exiled Louis-Philippe declaring that he had given way to *une insur-*

rection morale, and King Wilhelm of Württemberg excusing himself to the Russian minister at Stuttgart, one Gorchakov, with the words: '*Je ne puis pas monter à cheval contre les idées.*' And Namier calls his magnificent essay, 'The Revolution of the Intellectuals'.

1989 also erupted out of celebrations of 'forty years of peace and stability in Europe'. Remember NATO's fortieth anniversary in May? With the 'Yalta Europe', as with the 'Vienna Europe' in the previous century, the question was always: peace and stability *for whom*? Ordinary men and women in Central and Eastern Europe felt the rough edge of both. Here too, a stricter arithmetic might reduce the forty years to thirty-three, for perhaps it was only after crushing the Hungarian revolution of 1956 that Soviet leaders could be quite sure the West would not intervene militarily to disturb this peace—carefully preserved on a counter-revolutionary basis.

A revolution born as much of hopes as of discontents? Yes, again. To be sure, the economic 'discontents' were there, overwhelmingly in Poland and Romania, persistently, though less dramatically, elsewhere. In this connection, the historian Fritz Stern has aptly recalled Mirabeau's declaration on the eve of the French Revolution: 'The nation's deficit is the nation's treasure.' Substitute 'hard currency debt' for 'deficit' and you have one of the main reasons why it was Poland and Hungary that led the field in the first half of 1989. But, unlike in Poland in August 1980, it was not a turn of the economic screw that precipitated mass popular protest in any East European country in 1989. It was political hopes—and outrage at the repression with which the local regimes attempted to curb those hopes.

Like 1848, this, too, might be called a 'revolution of the

intellectuals'. To be sure, the renewed flexing of workers' muscle in two strike-waves in 1988 was what finally brought Poland's communists to the first Round Table of 1989. To be sure, it was the masses on the streets in demonstrations in all the other East European countries that brought the old rulers down. But the politics of the revolution were not made by workers or peasants. They were made by intellectuals: the playwright Václav Havel, the medievalist Bronisław Geremek, the Catholic editor Tadeusz Mazowiecki, the painter Bärbel Bohley in Berlin, the conductor Kurt Masur in Leipzig, the philosophers János Kis and Gaspár Miklós Támás in Budapest, the engineering professor Petre Roman and the poet Mircea Dinescu in Bucharest. History has outdone Shelley, for poets were the acknowledged legislators of this world. The crowds on Wenceslas Square chanted, 'Long live the students! Long live the actors!' And the sociology of the opposition forums (New, Democratic, Civic), parties and parliamentary candidates was distinctly comparable with that of the Frankfurt Parliament or the Slav Congress at Prague. *Hundert zwanzig Professoren* . . .

As in 1848, the common denominator was ideological. The inner history of these revolutions is that of a set of ideas whose time had come, and a set of ideas whose time had gone. At first glance this may seem a surprising statement. For had not the ideology ceased to be an active force many years before? Surely the rulers no longer believed a word of the guff they spouted, nor expected their subjects to believe it, nor even expected their subjects to believe that they, the rulers, believed it? This is probably true in most cases, although who knows what an old man like Erich Honecker, a communist from his earliest youth, still genuinely believed? (One must never underestimate the human capacity for self-deception.)

Yet one of the things these revolutions showed, *ex post facto*, is just how important the residual veil of ideology still was. Few rulers are content to say simply: 'We have the Gatling gun and you do not!' 'We hold power because we hold power.' Ideology provided a residual legitimation, perhaps also enabling the rulers, and their polit-bureaucratic servants, at least partly to deceive themselves about the nature of their own rule. At the same time, it was vital for the semantic occupation of the public sphere. The combination of censorship and a nearly complete Party-state monopoly of the mass media provided the army of semantic occupation; ideology, in the debased, routinized form of newspeak, was its ammunition. However despised and un-credible these structures of organized lying were, they continued to perform a vital blocking function. They no longer mobilized anyone, but they did still prevent the public articulation of shared aspirations and common truths.

What is more, by demanding from the ordinary citizen seemingly innocuous semantic signs of outward conformity, the system managed somehow to implicate them in it. It is easy now to forget that until almost the day before yesterday, almost everyone in East Germany and Czechoslovakia was living a double life: systematically saying one thing in public and another in private. This was a central theme of the essayistic work of Václav Havel over the last decade and one he movingly returned to in his 1990 New Year's address as president. The worst thing was, he said, the 'devastated moral environment. We are all morally sick, because we all got used to saying one thing and thinking another.' And: 'All of us have become accustomed to the totalitarian system, accepted

it as an unalterable fact and therefore kept it running ...
None of us is merely a victim of it, because all of us helped
to create it together.' The crucial 'line of conflict', he
wrote earlier, did not run between people and state, but
rather through the middle of each individual 'for everyone in his or her own way is both a victim and a supporter
of the system.' A banner I saw above the altar in an East
Berlin church vividly expressed the same basic thought.
It said: 'I am Cain *and* Abel.'

In order to understand what it meant for ordinary
people to stand in those vast crowds in the city squares
of Central Europe, chanting their own, spontaneous
slogans, you have first to make the imaginative effort to
understand what it feels like to pay this daily toll of
public hypocrisy. As they stood and shouted together,
these men and women were not merely healing divisions
in their society; they were healing divisions in themselves. Everything that had to do with the word, with the
press, with television, was of the first importance to these
crowds. The semantic occupation was as offensive to
them as military occupation; cleaning up the linguistic
environment as vital as cleaning up the physical environment. The long queue every morning in Wenceslas
Square, lining up patiently in the freezing fog for a
newspaper called *The Free Word*, was, for me, one of the
great symbolic pictures of 1989.

The motto of the year—and not just in Czechoslovakia
—was *Pravda Vitězí*, the old Hussite slogan, adopted by
Masaryk, 'Truth shall prevail,' or, in the still more
ancient Latin, *Magna est veritas et praevalebit*. As one
talks in English of a 'moment of truth' for some undertaking, so this was a year of truth for communism. There
is a real sense in which these regimes lived by the word
and perished by the word.

For what, after all, happened? A few thousands, then tens of thousands, then hundreds of thousands went on to the streets. They spoke a few words. 'Resign!' they said. 'No more shall we be slaves!' 'Free elections!' 'Freedom!' And the walls of Jericho fell. And with the walls, the communist parties simply crumbled. At astonishing speed. By the end of 1989, the Hungarian Socialist Workers' Party had split in two, with the majority of its members leaving for good. In January 1990, the Polish United Workers' Party followed suit. Within three months, East Germany's Socialist Unity Party lost its leading role, its name, and at least half its members. The inner decay of these parties recalled the remark of a German poet in 1848: 'Monarchy is dead, though monarchs still live.'

With the single, signal exception of Romania, these revolutions were also remarkable for the almost complete lack of violence. Like Solidarity in 1980-81 they were that historical contradiction-in-terms, 'peaceful revolution'. No bastilles were stormed, no guillotines erected. Lamp-posts were used only for street-lighting. Romania alone saw tanks and firing squads. Elsewhere the only violence was that used at the outset by police. The young demonstrators in East Berlin and Prague laid candles in front of the police, who responded with truncheons. The Marseillaise of 1989 said not *'aux armes, citoyens'* but *'aux bougies, citoyens'*. The rationale and tradition of non-violence can be found in the history of all the democratic oppositions of East Central Europe throughout the 1980s. Partly it was pragmatic: the other side had all the weapons. But it was also ethical. It was a statement about how things should be. They wanted to start as they intended to go on. History, said Adam Michnik, had taught them that those who start

139

by storming bastilles will end up building their own.

Yet almost as remarkable, historically speaking, was the lack (so far, and Romania plainly excepted) of major *counter*-revolutionary violence. The police behaved brutally in East Germany up to and notably on the state's fortieth anniversary, 7 October, and in Czechoslovakia up to and notably on 17 November. In Poland the systematic deployment of counter-revolutionary force lasted over seven years, from the declaration of a 'state of war' on 13 December 1981 to the spring of 1989. But once the revolutions (or, in Poland and Hungary, 'refolutions') were under way, there was an amazing lack of coercive countermeasures. The communist rulers said, like King Wilhelm of Württemberg, 'I cannot mount on horseback against ideas.' But one is bound to ask: why not? Much of the modern history of Central Europe consisted precisely in rulers mounting on horseback against ideas. Much of the contemporary history of Central Europe, since 1945, consists in rulers mounting tanks against ideas. Until 1989 the most fitting motto for any history of this region was not 'Pravda Vitězí' but some lines from the nineteenth-century Polish poet, Cyprian Norwid:

> *Colossal armies, valiant generals,*
> *Police-secret, open, and of sexes two—*
> *Against whom have they joined together?*
> *Against a few ideas ... nothing new!*

So why was it different in 1989? Three reasons may be suggested. They might be labelled 'Gorbachev', 'Helsinki' and 'Tocqueville'. The new line in Soviet policy, christened by Gennady Gerasimov on 25 October the Sinatra doctrine—'I had it my way' as he actually misquoted the famous line—rather than the Brezhnev doctrine, was self-evidently essential. In East Germany, Moscow not only made it plain to the leadership that Soviet troops were not available for purposes of domestic repression, but also, it seems, went out of its way to let it be known—to the West, but also to the population concerned—that this was its position. In Czechoslovakia, the Soviet Union helped the revolution along by a nicely timed retrospective condemnation of the 1968 Warsaw Pact invasion. Throughout East Central Europe, the people at last derived some benefit from their ruling élites' chronic dependency on the Soviet Union, for, deprived of the Soviet Kalashnikov-crutch, those élites did not have another leg to stand on. Romania was the exception that proves the rule. It is no accident that it was precisely in the state for so long most *in*dependent of Moscow that the resistance of the security arm of the powers-that-were was most fierce, bloody and prolonged.

None the less, the factor 'Gorbachev' alone does not suffice to explain why these ruling élites did not more vigorously deploy their own, still formidable police and security forces in a last-ditch defence of their own power and privilege. Is it too fanciful to suggest that the constant, persistent harping of the West on certain international norms of domestic conduct, the East European leaders' yearning for international respectability, and the sensed linkage between this and the hard currency credits they so badly needed, in short, the factor 'Helsinki', played at least some part in staying the hands of those who might otherwise have given the order to shoot?

Yet none of this would have stopped them if they had still been convinced of their right to rule. The third, and perhaps the ultimately decisive factor, is that characteristic of revolutionary situations described by Alexis de

Tocqueville more than a century ago: the ruling élite's loss of belief in its own right to rule. A few kids went on the streets and threw a few words. The police beat them. The kids said: You have no right to beat us! And the rulers, the high and mighty, replied, in effect: Yes, we have no right to beat you. We have no right to preserve our rule by force. The end no longer justifies the means!

In fact the ruling élites, and their armed servants, distinguished themselves by their comprehensive unreadiness to stand up in any way for the things in which they had so long claimed to believe, and their almost indecent haste to embrace the things they had so long denounced as 'capitalism' and 'bourgeois democracy'. All over Eastern Europe there was the quiet flap of turning coats: one day they denounced Wałęsa, the next they applauded him; one day they embraced Honecker, the next they imprisoned him; one day they vituperated Havel, the next they elected him president.

1848 was called the Springtime of Nations or the Springtime of Peoples: the *Völkerfruhling, wiosna ludów*. The revolutionaries, in all the lands, spoke in the name of 'the people'. But the international solidarity of 'the people' was broken by conflict between nations, old and new, while the domestic solidarity of 'the people' was broken by conflict between social groups—what came to be known as 'classes'. 'Socialism and nationalism, as mass forces, were both the product of 1848,' writes A.J.P. Taylor. And for a century after 1848, until the communist deep freeze, central Europe was a battlefield of nations and classes.

Of what, or of whom, was 1989 the springtime? Of 'the people'? But in what sense? *'Wir sind das Volk,'* said the first great crowds in East Germany: we are the people.

142

But within a few weeks they were saying '*Wir sind EIN Volk*': we are one nation. In Poland, Hungary, Czechoslovakia, Romania, the crowds were a sea of national flags, while the people raised their voice to sing old national hymns. In Hungary and Romania they cut the communist symbols out of the centre of their flags. In East Germany there were, at first, no flags, no hymns. But gradually the flags came out, plain stripes of red, black and gold without the GDR hammer and dividers in the middle: the flag of Western—and before that of united—Germany.

In every Western newspaper commentary on Eastern Europe one now invariably reads that there is a grave danger of something called 'nationalism' reviving in this region. But what on earth does this mean? Does it mean that people are again proud to be Czech, Polish, Hungarian or, for that matter, German? That hearts lift at sight of the flag and throats tighten when they sing the national anthem?

Patriotism is not nationalism. Rediscovered pride in your own nation does not necessarily imply hostility to other nations. These movements were all, without exception, patriotic. They were not all nationalist. Indeed, in their first steps most of the successor regimes were markedly less nationalist than their communist predecessors. The Mazowiecki government in Poland adopted a decisively more liberal and enlightened approach to both the Jewish and the German questions than any previous government, indeed drawing criticism, on the German issue, from the communist-nationalists. In his first public statement as President, Václav Havel made a special point of thanking 'all Czechs, Slovaks and members of other nationalities'. His earlier remark on television that Czechoslovakia owes the Germans an apology for the post-war expulsion of the Sudeten Germans was fiercely criticized by—the communists. In Romania, the revolution began with the ethnic Romanian inhabitants of Timişoara making common cause with their ethnic Hungarian fellow-citizens. It would require very notable exertions for the treatment of the German and Hungarian minorities in post-revolutionary Romania to be worse than it was under Nicolae Ceauşescu.

Of course there are counter-examples. One of the nastier aspects of the German revolution was the excesses of popular support for a Party-government campaign against Polish 'smugglers and profiteers', and abuse of visiting black students and Vietnamese *Gastarbeiter*. In Hungarian opposition politics, the fierce infighting between the Hungarian Democratic Forum and the Free Democrats was not without an ethnic undertone, with some members of the former questioning the 'Hungarian-ness' of some members of the latter, who replied with charges of anti-Semitism. Thousands of Bulgarians publicly protested against the new government giving the Turkish-Muslim minority its rights.

If one looks slightly further ahead, there are obviously potential conflicts over other remaining minorities: notably the Hungarians in Romania, the Romanians in the Soviet Union (Moldavia), the Germans in Poland, Romania and the Soviet Union, and gypsies in several countries. There are the potential political uses of anti-Semitism. There is the difficulty of finding a combination of Czecho- and -Slovakia fully satisfactory to both Slovaks and Czechs. And there are the outstanding frontier questions, above all that of the post-1945 German-Polish frontier on the Oder-Neisse line.

Yet compared with Central Europe in 1848 or 1918/19

this is a relatively short list. Most nations have states, and have got used to their new frontiers. Ethnically the map is far more homogenous than it was in 1848 or 1918: as Ernest Gellner has observed, it is now a picture by Modigliani rather than Kokoschka. (The main artists were, of course, Hitler and Stalin: their brushes, war, deportation and mass murder.) National and ethnic conflicts may grow again both between and within these states, as they did in Eastern Europe before the last war, especially if their economic situation deteriorates. Or those national and ethnic conflicts may progressively be alleviated, as were those of Western Europe after the last war, especially if these countries' economic situation improves in a process of integration into a larger European common market and community. We shall see. But the historical record must show that 1989 was not a year of acute national and ethnic conflict in Eastern Europe west of the Soviet frontier. Quite the reverse: it was a year of solidarity both within and between nations. At the end of the year, symbolic and humanitarian support for the people(s) of Romania came from all the self-liberated states of East Central Europe. A springtime of nations is not *necessarily* a springtime of 'nationalism'.

In any case, what was most striking was not the language of nationhood. That was wholly predictable. What was striking was the other ideas and words that, so to speak, shared the top billing. One of these was 'society'. In Poland, a country often stigmatized as 'nationalist', the word most often used to describe the people as opposed to the authorities was not 'nation'; it was *społeczeństwo*, society. In Czechoslovakia the word 'society' was used in a similar way, though less frequently, and here it could not simply be a synonym or euphemism for 'nation' because it covered two nations. In

145

both cases, it was as meaningful to talk of social self-determination as it was to talk of national self-determination. Everywhere stress was laid on the self-conscious unity of intelligentsia, workers and peasants. Of course in part this unity was created by the common enemy. When communist power had been broken, and real parliamentary politics began, then conflicting social interests were robustly articulated. Thus probably the most distinctive and determined group in the new Polish parliament was not communists or Solidarity, left or right, but peasant-farmers from all parties, combining and conspiring to advance their sectional interests.

None the less, the social divisions were nothing like as deep as in the nineteenth- or early twentieth-century, and they did not undercut the revolutions. There is an historical irony here. For in large measure communism created the social unity which contributed decisively to the end of communism. The combination of deliberate levelling, and unintended absurdities, resulted in a distribution of wealth throughout most of society that was not so much egalitarian as higgledy-piggledy. A professor would earn less than a miner, an engineer less than a peasant-farmer. A plumber with a few dollars or Deutschmarks would be better off than a prince without hard currency. A worker lived in the same house as a doctor, an engineer or a writer: and the ground plan of their apartments was almost certainly identical, even if the décor differed. At the same time, they were all united by consciousness of the one great divide between the communist upper/ruling class, the *nomenklatura*, and all the rest. In all these countries the latter were 'them': *oni* (a word made famous by Teresa Torańska's book of interviews with Polish Stalinists), the *Bonzen*. 'They' were identified by their clothes, their black curtained cars, their special hospitals and shops, their language and their behaviour. When the dense crowds in Prague were asked to clear a path for an ambulance, they did so chanting, 'We are not like them! We are not like them!'

At the same time, there was a remarkably high level of popular political awareness. Again, this was partly a result of the system. Everyone had at least a basic education, and from the earliest years that education was highly politicized. Many people reacted against this politicization with a determined retreat into private life, and an almost programmatic apoliticism. But because of the politicization of education, and the ubiquity of ideology, no one could be in any doubt that words and ideas mattered, having real consequences for everyday life.

A concept that played a central role in opposition thinking in the 1980s was that of 'civil society'. 1989 was the springtime of societies aspiring to be civil. Ordinary men and women's rudimentary notion of what it meant to build a civil society might not satisfy the political theorist. But some such notion was there, and it contained several basic demands. There should be forms of association, national, regional, local, professional, which would be voluntary, authentic, democratic and, first and last, not controlled or manipulated by the Party or Party-state. People should be 'civil': that is, polite, tolerant, and, above all, non-violent. Civil and civilian. The idea of citizenship had to be taken seriously.

Communism managed to poison many words from the mainstream of European history—not least, as this book has repeatedly indicated, the word 'socialism'. But somehow it did not manage to poison the words 'citizen' and 'civic', even though it used them, too, in perverted ways: for example, in appeals to 'civic responsiblity' meaning, 'Keep quiet and let us deal with these troublesome students.' Why it did not manage to poison those words is an interesting question—to which I have no ready answer—but the fact is that when Solidarity's parliamentarians came to give their group a name, they called it the *Citizens'* Parliamentary Club; the Czech movement called itself the *Civic* Forum; and the opposition groups in the GDR started by describing themselves as *Bürgerinitiativen*, that is, citizens' or civic initiatives. (In the East German case, the actual word was probably imported from West Germany, but the fact remains that they chose this rather than another term.) And the language of citizenship was important in all these revolutions. People had had enough of being mere components in a deliberately atomized society: they wanted to be citizens, individual men and women with dignity and responsibility, with rights but also with duties, freely associating in civil society.

There is one last point about the self-description of the revolution which is perhaps worth a brief mention. As Ralf Dahrendorf has observed, Karl Marx played on the ambiguity of the German term *bürgerliche Gesellschaft*, which could be translated either as civil society or as *bourgeois* society. Marx, says Dahrendorf, deliberately conflated the two 'cities' of modernity, the fruits of the Industrial and the French Revolutions, the bourgeois and the citoyen. I thought of this observation when a speaker in one of the mass rallies in Leipzig called for solidarity with the *bürgerliche Bewegung* in Czechoslovakia. The bourgeois movement! But on reflection there seems to me a deeper truth in that apparent malapropism. For what most of the opposition movements throughout East Central Europe and a large part of 'the people' supporting them were in effect saying was: Yes, Marx is right, the two things are intimately connected—and we want both! Civil rights and property rights, economic freedom and political freedom, financial independence and intellectual independence, each supports the other. So, yes, we want to be citizens, but we also want to be middle-class, in the senses that the majority of citizens in the more fortunate half of Europe are middle-class. We want to be *Bürger* AND *bürgerlich*! Tom Paine, but also Thomas Mann.

So it was a springtime of nations, but not necessarily of nationalism; of societies, aspiring to be civil; and above all, of citizens.

The springtime of citizens has already changed the face of Europe. What seemed only possible at the beginning of 1989 seemed certain at the beginning of 1990. There would be a new Europe, for which the term 'Yalta' would no longer be an appropriate shorthand. This Europe would have a different place for the countries formerly described as East European, and, at the very least, a less divided Germany.

1848 ended badly because of the combination of internal and external forces of reaction; but the external ones were decisive. No comparable external forces of reaction were visible at the beginning of 1990. The Prussians were making their own revolution, not crushing those of their neighbours. Austrians were not repressing the Hungarian reform-revolution, but helping it along. And the Russians? Here the transformation was miraculous, to the point where senior American and British officials indicated that they might actually welcome a Soviet military intervention to smash the Securitate death squads in Romania. But no, for Romania, as for Czechoslovakia, Hungary, Poland and Bulgaria, Soviet leaders and commentators from

149

Gorbachev down assumed a saintly expression and said they would never dream of interfering in the internal affairs of another sovereign state.

Yet the popular movement for national and social self-determination did not stop neatly at the western frontier of the Soviet Union. What happened in Eastern Europe directly encouraged the Baltic States, not to mention the Romanians of Soviet Moldavia. And what if the political earth began to move in the Ukraine? At the beginning of 1990 it was therefore all too possible to imagine some backlash or reversal inside the Soviet Union. But it seemed reasonable to doubt whether even a conservative-military leadership in Moscow would attempt to use armed force to restore Russian domination west of the Soviet frontiers of 1945. Would they not have more than enough on their hands trying to preserve the empire inside the post-war Soviet frontiers? Logically, if they invaded one East European country they should now invade them all. And then, what would they 'restore'? The shattered humpty-dumpties that were yesterday's East European communist parties? Obviously a reversal inside the Soviet Union would make life much less comfortable in the new Europe, and directly affect developments in a Germany still partly occupied by Soviet troops. But it would not in itself suffice to turn the map back to what it was before 1989.

About this new Europe there are countless questions to be asked, of which the most obviously pressing is: how can the West help the transition of formerly communist states into liberal democracies? I ask myself a less obvious question: not 'How can we help them?' but 'How might they help us?' What, if anything, can these nearly hundred million Europeans, with their forty years of hard experience, bring to the new Europe, and to us in the West? The Czechs were delighted to point out that '89 is '68 turned upside down. But one of the notable differences between '68 and '89 was the comparative lack of Western intellectuals discovering, in these exotic regions, new utopias, 'socialism with a human face' and the fabled Third Way.

Of course there is a whole kaleidoscope of new parties, programmes and trends, and it is little short of impudence to subsume them in one 'message'. Yet if you look at what these diverse parties are really saying about the basic questions of politics, economics, law and international relations, there is a remarkable underlying consensus. In politics they are all saying: there is no 'socialist democracy,' there is only democracy. And by democracy they mean multi-party, parliamentary democracy as practised in contemporary Western, Northern and Southern Europe. They are all saying: there is no 'socialist legality', there is only legality. And by that they mean the rule of law, guaranteed by the constitutionally anchored independence of the judiciary. They are all saying, and for the left this is perhaps the most important statement: there is no 'socialist economics', there is only economics. And economics means not a socialist market economy but a social market economy. Not Ota Šik but Ludwig Erhard. Of course there are grave differences in these countries between, for example, Friedmanites and Hayekites. A good word might even be heard for Keynes. But the general direction is absolutely plain: towards an economy whose basic engine of growth is the market, with extensive private ownership of the means of production, distribution and exchange. The transition to such a system poses unique problems, for which original solutions will have to be found. In most of these countries there is still widespread

151

support for relatively egalitarian distribution of the wealth thus created, and for a strong welfare state. But the basic model, in the three essentials of politics, law and economics, is something between the real existing Switzerland and the real existing Sweden.

Sweden—or, as one leading Soviet economist carefully stressed, *southern* Sweden—now seems to be the accepted ideal for virtually everyone who styles themself a socialist from Berlin to Vladivostok. But if Marx came back to earth, would he not describe the dominant mode of production in Sweden as capitalist? In other words, the fundamental argument from the left seems no longer to be about the best way to produce wealth, only about the best way to distribute it. (The more fundamental critique of the successful forms of production comes from Greens rather than socialists.)

For purely practical and historical reasons, the state will clearly play a larger part in most formerly East European countries than in most West European countries, for some years to come. But this does not necessarily mean that people will want it to. On the contrary, having had so much state interference for so long, they might decide they want as little of it as possible. Public opinion polls and sociological surveys are not much use here, since most people have only just begun to think about these issues, let alone to confront them in the harsh reality of economic transition. The proof of the pudding will be in the eating. Among the intellectuals who have begun to confront these issues there is, it seems to me, rather an opposite danger: that of regarding the free market as a cure for all ills, social and political as well as economic. Hence the popularity of Hayek. One might almost say that the free market is the latest Central European utopia.

It is easy now to forget that communism claimed to have found not only new and better forms of politics, law and economics, but also a new and better way of organizing relations between states. This new way was called 'socialist internationalism', and counterposed to 'bourgeois nationalism'. What we have seen in practice is the rise of socialist nationalism and bourgeois internationalism. There are many examples of bourgeois internationalism—G7, OECD, IMF, NATO, GATT— but in the perspective of European history the most dramatic is the European Community. Now there are proposals, too numerous even to list, for new forms of inter-state relations in the former Eastern Europe. To give but one example, leading Polish politicians have revived the idea of a confederation of Poland and Czecho-slovakia. But if you ask what is the underlying model for the new relations between these states, and for the resolution of their outstanding national, ethnic and economic conflicts, then the answer is clear. The model is the European Community.

This means not only that they would like to join the present EC, as fully as possible and as soon as possible. It also means that they hope their outstanding historic conflicts and enmities can be overcome in the same way that, say, those between France and Germany have been overcome. This is true, it seems to me, even of those groups that would not explicitly acknowledge the EC as a model. Certainly, you have to go far in Western Europe to find such enthusiastic 'Europeans'—that is, support-ers of a supranational community called Europe—as you will find at every turn in Eastern Europe. Travelling to and fro between the two halves of the divided continent, I have sometimes thought that the real divide is between those (in the West) who have Europe and those (in the

East) who believe in it. And everywhere, in all the lands, the phrase people use to sum up what is happening is 'the return to Europe'.

Yet what, to repeat the question, can these enthusiasts bring to the new Europe? If I am right in my basic analysis, they can offer no fundamentally new ideas on the big questions of politics, economics, law or international relations. The ideas whose time has come are old, familiar, well-tested ones. (It is the new ideas whose time has passed.) So is all they have to offer us their unique, theoretically intriguing but practically burdensome problems? Do they come like mendicants to the door bearing only chronicles of wasted time? Or might they have, under their threadbare cloaks, some hidden treasures?

Travelling through this region over the last decade, I have found treasures: examples of great moral courage and intellectual integrity; comradeship, deep friendship, family life; time and space for serious conversation, music, literature, not disturbed by the perpetual noise of our media-driven and obsessively telecommunicative world; Christian witness in its original and purest form; more broadly, qualities of relations between men and women of very different backgrounds, and once bitterly opposed faiths—an ethos of solidarity. Here the danger of sentimental idealization is acute, for the privileged visitor enjoys these benefits without paying the costs. There is no doubt that, on any quantitative or utilitarian reckoning, the costs have been far higher than the benefits. Yet it would be even more wrong to pretend that these treasures were not real. They were. And for me the question of questions after 1989 is: What if any of these good things will survive liberation? Was the community *only* a community of fate, a *Schicksalsgemeinschaft*? Were these *just* the uses of adversity?

Even if there is no reversal in the Soviet Union, no violent backlash or illiberal turn in this or that East European country, won't these treasures simply be swept away in the rush—the all too understandable rush—for affluence? As a Hungarian friend wryly remarked: 'I have survived forty years of communism, but I'm not sure that I'll survive one year of capitalism.' And this will not just be the atomizing impact of developed consumerism, one of the most potent weapons known to man. It will be the still rougher and more traumatic impact of the attempted transition from a planned to a market economy, with all the associated blows of un-employment, dislocation and injustice.

Wishful thinking helps no one. You can, alas, paint with a rather high degree of analytical plausibility a quite dark picture of the prospect for the former Eastern Europe in the 1990s: a prospect in which the post-communist future looks remarkably like the pre-communist past, less Central Europe than *Zwischen-europa*, a dependent intermediate zone of weak states, national prejudice, inequality, poverty and *Schlamassel*. 1989 might then appear, to participants and historians, as just one brief shining moment between the sufferings of yesterday and those of tomorrow.

This fate is not inevitable. Whether it can be avoided depends to a very significant degree on the commitment and ingenuity of the West in general, Western Europe in particular, and above all on West Germany—or rather, to put it in terms more appropriate to the new Europe, on a Germany remaining Western.

Yet even if the darker prospect were to be realized, something would remain, at least in memory, in culture, in spirit. At the very least the Europeans from over there would have offered us, with a clarity and firmness born of

155

bitter experience, a restatement of the value of what we already have, of old truths and tested models, of the three essentials of liberal democracy and the European Community as the one and only, real existing common European home. Intellectually, dare I say spiritually, '1989' in Eastern Europe is a vital complement to '1992' in Western Europe.

'*Litwo! Ojczyzno moja! ty jesteś jak zdrowie,*' begins the most famous of all Polish poems, Adam Mickiewicz's 'Pan Tadeusz':

> *Lithuania, my fatherland, thou art like health;*
> *How much we should value thee, he alone learns,*
> *Who has lost thee.*

If we put in place of 'Lithuania' the word 'Europe', we may have the deepest lesson of that year of wonders, '89.

Acknowledgments

For this book, thanks especially to Bill Buford, Tim Adams and Angus MacKinnon at Granta Books; Robert Silvers and the *New York Review*; Charles Moore and the *Spectator*; George Schöpflin and Rudolf Tőkés on Hungary; Ralf Dahrendorf and colleagues at St Antony's.

GRANTA BOOKS

TIMOTHY GARTON ASH

THE USES OF ADVERSITY

Ten years ago, Timothy Garton Ash came to East Berlin to find out from the archives what the Berliners had done under Hitler. Instead he found out—from the streets—what the Berliners were doing under Honecker. He wrote about what he saw—in German—and the authorities protested. When he tried to return to East Berlin, he was turned back. He went to Poland and wrote a history of Solidarity. It was translated into Polish and he was blacklisted at the frontier. He went to Prague to attend a Charter 77 meeting, but was met instead by the secret police.

Ten years ago, Timothy Garton Ash began to discover Central Europe. *The Uses of Adversity* records what he found.

'A passionate case for the liberation and cultural survival of Central Europe, pursued with wit and discrimination. Since the book came out in September, events have nudged its status up from Useful to Essential.'
Anthony Lane, *Independent*

'A collection of brilliant articles which not only describe but participate in the current metamorphosis of the Eastern European countries, Timothy Garton Ash's excellent *The Uses of Adversity* shows that a British writer can still take the world for scope.'
Clive James, *Observer*

Hardback, £13.95 ISBN 0 140 14202 9
Paperback, £5.99 ISBN 0 140 14018 2